Managing to

GW00492971

Sir John Harvey-Jones is one of Britain's
best-known and admired businessmen. He
was chairman of ICI from 1982 to 1987.
Amongst his wide-ranging interests, he is
currently chairman of *The Economist* and a
non-executive director of Grand
Metropolitan.

Sir John's television series,
Troubleshooter, with its clear-sighted look at
ailing British companies, became a national
talking point in the late eighties and as
chairman of ICI he topped the *Sunday
Times* poll of captains of industry five years
running. His most recent book with
Heinemann, *Getting It Together*, was
published in 1991 and became a number
one bestseller. The *Sunday Times* said of it,
'Sir John is that rare animal, a businessman
who makes business exciting . . . No
businessman has ever written a memoir like
it' and the *Sunday Telegraph* called it
'charming and inspiring'.

Also by Sir John Harvey-Jones
*available from Mandarin Paperbacks

Making It Happen
Getting It Together*

Managing to Survive

John Harvey-Jones

Mandarin

A Mandarin Paperback
MANAGING TO SURVIVE

First published in Great Britain 1993
by William Heinemann Ltd
This edition published 1993
by Mandarin Paperbacks
an imprint of Reed Consumer Books Ltd
Michelin House, 81 Fulham Road, London SW3 6RB
and Auckland, Melbourne, Singapore and Toronto

A CIP catalogue record for this title
is available from the British Library
ISBN 0 7493 1502 4

Printed and bound in Great Britain
by Cox & Wyman Ltd, Reading, Berkshire

To my much loved Gaby,
without whose collaboration and endless hard work
none of my books would be possible.

1 Can You Manage in the Nineties?

During my life in industry I have been aware of a different perception of management style for each decade that I have been in the business, despite the obvious fact that the external characteristics within which we were all operating during those decades were wildly different. For example, when I first started in industry in the fifties, the attractions of work measurement and method study as a means of improving productivity seemed almost like a philosopher's stone, even though the ideas had been around since the early twenties. During the 1960s there was an almost immediate shift to a different sort of fashion. There seemed to be a common belief that everything could be measured, and that, if only the accountancy systems were better and we embraced such concepts as discounted cash flow, success would automatically follow. The 1970s were the period when we discovered that concentrating on methods and systems somehow didn't seem to make the expected breakthroughs, and that people actually had feelings and beliefs of their own and social science came back in fashion. The 1980s were typified by their optimism, belief in expansion and the confidence that market forces would overcome the inflationary and other characteristics which had been such a bane of life in the seventies – and they could barely be more different than the nineties look.

I am bound to admit that I played a full part in each of these management fashions and, when I look back on my own management development, it is not hard to see that, as each of these ideas came and went, each of them left a residue in my beliefs about management in general. It has always fascinated me that management fashions seem to spread across the world with the speed of light, whereas transferring technology appears to be an extraordinarily difficult task to achieve. There can seldom have been a period when there were more people, including myself, writing management books, or more people becoming interested in the theories of management. The difficulty is that there can never be any single correct solution for any management problem, or any all-embracing system which will carry one through a particular situation or period of time. Most ideas on management have been around for a very long time, and the skill of the manager consists in knowing them all and, rather as he might choose the appropriate golf club for a specific situation, choosing the particular ideas which are most appropriate for the position and time in which he finds himself.

The manager, in whatever field he or she operates, has to manage in the environment in which he finds himself. Macro-economic and geo-economic forces affect everyone. No one is impervious to the effects of Japanese economic endeavour and power, any more than anyone can ignore the existence of the computer and information technology. Moreover, management, above everything else, is about people. It is about the accomplishment of ends and aims by the efforts of groups of people working together. The people and their individual hopes and skills are the greatest variable and the most important one. This has always been the case, but for a whole variety of reasons it is even more obvious now and is the key element for the future. Most of us who have been managers over the past years can recognise very clearly some of the management styles which pertained at various times in our careers. In my own case I can remember reacting to the decade of the accountant. This was the time when it was almost as though accountancy had just been invented. There was a curious belief that the figures themselves would automatically ensure appropriate action. There was even surprise when it was found that much of the action which did actually ensue took the form of argument about the derivation and accuracy of the numbers themselves. Nowadays, except in the communist countries, there is no manager who would not accept the need for management accounts and the role of numbers in making things happen. But there is a big difference of approach to the use of accounts and their role in management. They range from one extreme – the school of 'if you can't measure it, you can't manage it' – to the other extreme of using figures as a sort of calibration applied to the subjective factors on which the decision is based. It interests me that the Japanese use of management accounts is much closer to the latter approach. The big strategic decisions are taken on subjective factors and the numbers are used to check progress and define scale. Amongst the most celebrated examples was the insistence of Morita of Sony on producing the Walkman, against every piece of market research and set of figures that the extremely talented management at Sony were able to produce.

I have lived through other fashions – all of which have a continuing role to play in the complex business of management, but none of which has turned out to be quite the panacea we believed at the time. There was a time when the behavioural sciences were looked upon as the final word. Each of us studied Herzberg and Macgregor, and many of us went for sensitivity training. We studied group dynamics, which in their own way assumed predictable responses to predictable actions. We tried to learn, to listen and to read body language. We blamed our bad business decisions on our behavioural inadequacies – rather than lack of clarity of our aims or misinterpretation of our competitive position. When ICI found itself forced into selling petrol there were endless debates about whether we had handled our relationships with our suppliers, the oil companies, correctly – or whether a more behaviourist approach to our relationships could have maintained our position. The reality was brutally plain: the strategic interests of ICI and our suppliers were not in harmony and therefore a breakup was inevitable. An earlier realisation of this, and more attention to managing our way through, would have averted a good deal of pain for both ourselves and our suppliers. Do you remember the 'planning' years? Those days when battalions of our colleagues locked themselves away, with computers and calculators, to produce five-year forecasts we never achieved, and never owned. Weighty volumes of indigestible data were produced outlining – with surprising precision – our own actions in a world devoid of surprises, competition, and breaks in the continuum. There were many more, and there is still an absolute outpouring of ideas, simplistic solutions, and peddled systems – not to speak of business books such as this one. As the world around us becomes more complex, and the penalties for failure become more dire, it should not surprise us that we grasp for single-dose cures.

I am uncomfortably aware that all the foregoing may be thought to pour scorn on the very idea of management sciences and theories, which is not at all my intention. I believe that management is an art – and possibly one of the most difficult ones. Just as the artist constantly and consciously works to perfect his technique and to gain mastery of his relevant skills, so must the manager. Mere technical command of the skills does not, however, produce a virtuoso or a superb manager. It is that extra something which each of us brings from within ourselves that makes the difference – vision, judgement, awareness of the world around us, and responsiveness to that world, which leads to success. Managing is a matter of the mind and the character, and while there are great institutional managers, even they spend a lot of time and concentration thinking about their craft. The best managers combine pragmatism and practical experience with a continual absorption with the theoretical basis of their art. Nowadays with the explosion of business schools and students there is a constant outpouring of new research, new concepts and new theories. It is almost impossible to stay abreast of all this new thinking, but all of us who enjoy our craft are continuously dipping into books, papers and magazines, or attending conferences or courses to try to ensure that our thinking is kept fresh and alert. Like all other arts there are creative verities in the application of management, but there is also a continual, and essential, evolutionary development of new ideas. Paradoxically, I believe that management is more difficult and more demanding in the age of instant communication than it was one hundred years ago. In the last century there was no alternative to delegation and therefore much thought had to be given to the clarity of policy direction – for your people would be flying free. Nowadays it is perfectly possible (although in my view highly undesirable) to check, monitor and double guess every decision, virtually as it is taken. We all know the ease with which the chief executive is able to receive daily sales figures from the most remote part of his far-flung empire, and every one of us knows an individual who will ring up and ask why a particular sale has been made to a particular customer at a particular price. In the early days of computerisation, when every man or woman worth their salt delighted in crawling over pages of print-out, I remember being asked to explain why a particular price had been applied to a particular sale. Since the sale itself was minute in terms of our total turnover I had not even bothered to check the item myself, and yet such was the new power of the searchlight which shone upon our activities that it became a matter of absorbing interest to an extremely senior director, who, one would have thought, would have had many better things to do. This places real strains on the manager's self-discipline, courage, clarity of thought and trust in his subordinates – strains which, in times when it took three months to receive a reply to an instruction, were not there in that particular form.

I believe that the decade of the nineties is going to be a very different time from any we have so far experienced. The seeds of these differences have already germinated and are plain to see, even if the final outcome is not. It behoves all of us who are managers (and want to be better ones) to look at this array of seedlings and try to think our own way through this very different world in which we are likely to be operating. In the light of this we need to look at the skills we have – making sure we work on those which may be a bit rusty, and trying hard to acquire the ones we may not have. They will be different for each of us, not least because the same external conditions mean very different things to different businesses. A recession affects the business prospects for those involved in liquidation, or debt collecting, in a very different way from the effect it has on small undercapitalised businesses, caught in the middle of expansion, on borrowed money. A shift in exchange rates inevitably creates winners as well as losers – and so on. But they will also be different because every manager, and every group of people to be managed, is different. What works with one will not work with another, and the additional skills needed for an introverted individual may not be the same as those needed by his more outgoing colleague. There is no right or wrong in all of this. The only test of management, and it is a tough one, is success. But success comes more easily to those who study the world around them, and are continually updating their craft, than to those who try to repeat a formula that worked once in the past. The world is littered with failed former heroes, who were so intoxicated with a success that they failed to adapt to new circumstances and new demands. Disastrously, at the present time we are seeing two of the world's greatest companies struggling to adapt in an almost emergency manner to situations which have been building and visible for a long time. The idea that General Motors and IBM should simultaneously be having to undergo their current traumatic changes would have been unthinkable even ten years ago. However, it is largely because they have found it so difficult to adapt 'on the run' that they have found themselves in their present sorry situation.

So what about the nineties? Why, and in what ways, are they likely to be different, and to pose new challenges for which we must prepare? I am no futurologist, and indeed I distrust the genre. It is certainly possible to project present trends at differing rates – and to draw some surprising conclusions. But they are conclusions that seldom occur in real life because invariably other factors break the progression. There are, however, some things which are already clear, and the greatest of these is the rate and unpredictability of change. Much has been written on this subject, but without question the rate of change with which managers have to cope is the greatest of any period in my lifetime. It isn't only the rate, it is the vast variety of factors which affect business, which are all changing at the same time, which are going to make this decade such an exciting and different one. The rate of macro-economic change alone would be difficult to cope with, and the time-scale is far outside our own planning horizons. Who, for instance, in their five-year plan from 1990, allowed for war in the Gulf? Who, three years ago, foresaw the release of Central Europe from Soviet domination? Or, even eighteen months ago, the apparently irreconcilable economic travails of the Soviet Union? All of these unpredictable and unpredicted events change the world within which we operate. All have impacts so far reaching that they will affect practically all businesses in one way or another, and managers in practically every field.

Even if one takes an event which we have known about for over five years – namely 1992 and the single market – the end result is pretty much the same. There can never have been a more advertised and heralded event in economic history – a full five years of preparation, and endless exhortation, by Governments and press alike. How many managers have thought their way through these predicted changes, and allowed, in their strategic aims and intermediate plans, for the massively different ways of doing things that lie ahead? All of us are aware that 1992 foreshadows a heavy increase in competition. All of us know that it involves revolutionary changes in distribution costs. Most of us pay lip service to the view that it involves the restructuring of European industry. But restructuring is something that can happen to you, or that you can make happen to someone else. How many of us are trying to drive the restructuring of our industry to our own advantage?

The single market isn't something which happened at 00.01 on New Year's Eve in 1992. It has been evolving for some time, and will continue to change and develop for many years to come. So how many managers have looked fundamentally anew, with a blank sheet of paper, and decided how they are going to serve this massive single market? How many have looked overseas, to the USA for instance, and drawn lessons from there as to how we are likely to end up? How many are rationalising their manufacturing capabilities, shutting down peripheral factories on the European fringe to concentrate on a hub manufacturing presence? A splendid example of this sort of thinking is the action taken by the Coca-Cola company to shut down bottling plants in four countries and concentrate on one enormous one in France. I suggest that, for most of us, our speed of reaction to opportunity is a tithe of our speed of reaction to adversity. Yet our opportunity is someone else's adversity, and who gets there first all too often wins. Macro-economic change affects us all equally, but all too often we wait for others to take the initiative, and we assume too readily that competitors will react as we do. The reality is, of course, that they don't. Many managers make their own plans in a vacuum of knowledge and sometimes even a lack of interest in their competitors' capabilities and intentions. It isn't necessary to resort to illegal industrial espionage in order to make an intelligent assessment of your competitors' abilities or likely actions. Financial disclosure requirements, intelligence from the market-place, the trade press, are all constantly clamouring for your attention and yet all too often such matters are looked on as titillating gossip, rather than hard facts to be reacted to.

It is not trespassing on the futurologists' art to observe that the nineties are likely to be highly turbulent and unpredictable in the macro-economic sense. It seems unlikely that there will be a stable economic environment in the Middle East, Central Europe, or the Soviet Union in the immediate future. Add to that the list of problems facing the USA in terms of economic change, and even the internal pressures in Japan which are going to force further, and major, adjustments on that most adaptable of economies, and it's a brave or foolhardy business-man who makes a single-line five-year forecast. This is, of course, just one area where the forces for change are roaring around our ears, and I suggest that, on its own, it is wellnigh impossible to plan for.

Look, however, at what is happening to technology and new development. The technology available already far exceeds our ability to apply or to use it. Moreover, we have unlocked certain technological gates which are enabling us to expand our scientific understanding at an unprecedented rate. These changes, allied to changes in management thinking and competitive pressures, are flooding our markets with enabling devices and ideas faster than we can adapt to them. Over the past years I have met and talked with many of the world's leading information technology companies. I have yet to find one who would claim to be using, in their own operations, as much as sixty per cent of the technology available today. And remember that the available technology will double within the next five years. When do we catch up? And how? It should be borne in mind that an electronics engineer's training is outdated within less than ten years and he then needs a 'retread'. Management, organisations and the concepts of how we get things done and of what people do, are critically dependent on our use of technology.

It isn't only the fundamental development of technology that is moving so fast that it is opening doors of opportunity faster than we can appreciate. All of us are aware of the unbelievable speeding up there has been in applying technology to the market-place. Typically the time taken to produce a new product has been reduced by a factor of between four and ten. This change has critically affected our approach to management and the strategies for our businesses. We can no longer rely on a single success carrying us through for the decade or more. A successful product merely gives us a head start in the race, and our future will lie in producing improvements and variants, and targeting them into the market faster than our competition can. The classic example of this is the Sony Corporation and the Walkman – an idea of breathtaking apparent eccentricity, pushed through by Morita himself. Despite achieving a breakthrough in concept, and creating an entirely new need, Sony only stay in front by a constant stream of improvements and novel developments on the original concept. From the original idea of having a simple, portable player which would fit in the pocket, so that the individual need never be separated from their favourite diet of canned music, they have moved to ever more elaborate 'Walkpeople'. These have involved radio and tapes, and have now taken in concepts such as the Discman, so that one need never be separated from one's compact disc player – and now there are even portable videos. Moreover, Sony now produce a range of six or seven different models of Walkman, all with slightly different characteristics, but at very different prices!

Such a strategy places very different demands on management style and organisation than a single product strategy, where the only drive is to continuously reduce the cost. It is to this area, between technological change and management opportunity, that one can trace much of the current thinking of new management concepts. It is, moreover, the area where our track record is the poorest, and where I believe the nineties are going to punish those who do not think fundamentally about the problems.

Essentially our approach to technological advance has been to apply it to our old ways of doing things and to evolve the new ideas only slowly. Cast your mind back to the introduction of computers into businesses. Initially they were used as a means of mechanising clerical tasks, in order to reduce costs. Later it was realised that computers could control complex machinery better, and with less variability, than humans, so they were applied progressively to plant control purposes. Even today, and even amongst computer companies themselves, it is difficult to find examples where companies have seized the organisational and managerial opportunities opened to them by use of the computers. I know of some firms where the computer-aided design departments link directly with their sub-contractor's design department, so that they can develop a new product in parallel, and some that link directly with their supplier's computer-aided manufacture.

Technology has already started to attack some of yesterday's most cherished concepts. The economies of scale are less obvious and, most of us now realise, have to be measured against potential loss of flexibility and speed of response. Amongst the entrenched beliefs with which I grew up as a businessman, one of the most sacred cows was that the advantages would always go to the largest organisation, because the larger the scale and size of the plant, the lower would be the costs of production. The difficulty with this belief was that we built larger and larger plants, which were in fact less and less flexible and required us to hold larger and larger stocks. The trend was to look at one aspect of the cost – which was the all-up production cost per ton or unit, and it was this which led us to pursue scale, almost in its own right. It is interesting to note that now most of us are looking for flexibility: production lines which can produce many different models at the same time; machining centres which can machine any item or product; parallel production systems which gain in speed and time, although apparently sub-optimising in cost, are all developments which lie totally against the beliefs of yesterday. Sustainable competitive advantage through production technology is very difficult to achieve and transfer of such technology is very quick. The latest robots are available world-wide contemporaneously, due to the pressures and needs for global thinking. The effects of these changes in the needs of manufacturing are very far reaching. In the first place the cost of variety is sharply reduced, enabling competition to develop in unexpected ways. Some years ago the key concept was one of reducing variety in car models and styles. Today we see manufacturers continuously increasing the range of their products, in many cases for total production runs which would have been considered suicidal even five years ago.

We have seen some fundamental changes in the proportions of cost which are involved in the whole production function. In my early days in industry a production system where the cost of the people was under twenty per cent of the total cost was seen as being capital intensive, and was believed to impose different business pressures than those where the cost of the people was as high as fifty per cent. These beliefs were partly engendered because when demand fell it was possible to lay people off, and indeed in some industries, like the docks, people were hired solely for specific jobs. A capital intensive plant was seen as being inflexible, because most of the costs lay in the capital itself. These went on irrespective of the amount of product which was produced, and indeed only became tolerable if they were spread across a constant and very high production rate. More and more the competition lies in the use of capital, rather than in the cost of people. Typically, in fully robotised plants, the cost of the people directly employed in the plant – actually running it, moving things around and making sure that the plant works and so on – is well under ten per cent of the total production cost. While it is, of course, essential that the productivity of your workforce is continuously improved, nevertheless, the chance of gaining a world lead by reducing people costs from, say, six per cent to five per cent, is relatively small. The competitive advantage, therefore, comes more and more from the use that is made of the plant and machinery than in the actual operation of the production system itself. The competition lies in brain, in fact, rather than in brawn, and is increasingly in departments which, in some cases, were considered almost extraneous to business performance. Departments such as advertising, branding, research and development, distribution and accounting are the areas where the battle for competitive advantage is now joined. They are also the departments where the major costs of operating the business are centred, and it is on the focusing of these departments, and ensuring that they make the maximum contribution to the whole, that future battlegrounds lie. Even more fundamentally, as the cost of the people involved in production reduces as a proportion of the total cost, two things happen: increasingly, production itself becomes a fixed, rather than a variable cost, and the total competitive position of the product depends more and more on the skill with which what used to be called the 'overheads' are managed. The overheads, which hitherto were managed for functional performance as much as costs, are now the key area. Selling, advertising, distribution, research, development, costing and accounting departments are where the battle is joined.

These are amongst the reasons why I believe that the nineties are going to be the decade of management, and why I think the winners will be those who think radically, embrace change and create adaptable organisations that switch people on and release energy. After all there is no intrinsic reason why my robot, or my computer, should be any better or any worse than its Taiwanese competitor. The struggle of the nineties will be about what each of us does with the same tools, how we view our strategic aims and how we organise and motivate our people. In fact how we manage our businesses.

Which brings me to the third area of change with which we have to cope in the nineties. I refer to people and their aspirations. Every annual report by every chairman all over the world ends up by paying a tribute to 'our people – our greatest resource'. Yet boards of directors hardly ever take time out to look at the totality of the environment in which 'our greatest resource' works. Most boards take a look at the management development plans, the pay policy, the rates of staff turnover and, increasingly, albeit belatedly, at the effort and cost put into training. All of these things are important, and most of them are quantifiable in some way or other. But all of us who have worked for others know that they constitute only a relatively small part of the reasons we like or dislike our work, and give – or withhold – our best efforts.

I have been trying to develop the argument in this chapter that, for reasons of mass economic and technical change alone, the nineties are going to pose new and different management challenges. I have tried to demonstrate that success in meeting these challenges will depend, even more than in the past, on the way in which all of us are managed and motivated, and that the rewards of international success will go to those who are most successful in this field. But there is another aspect to all of this that we disregard at our peril. It is that people, their education, background, hopes and aspirations, are changing fundamentally and, by human standards, very fast. People's values and hopes work to a fairly long time-scale, which is why managing change is a job for the patient and the persistent. Perhaps because of this fact, allied to the notorious difficulty of communicating across generations, managers and leaders are continually surprised when younger people do not react in the same way as they did at a similar age. Women's liberation and the feminist movement have been with us for a very long time and yet only now are organisations realising that there is an enormous pressure for genuine career opportunities for women. Thank God there is, for I have never understood how we can expect to compete if we ignore, or fail to harness, half the brainpower in the country. Perhaps the reason that organisations have been so myopic about the different needs that women have in following a career, is that the majority of older managers are male. Successful managers in the nineties, as I have reiterated over and over again, will be those who have the flexibility to adapt their organisations and behaviour to the needs of their people rather than the reverse.

In their search for security the older generations accepted that they would go anywhere at the behest of their employer. We neither expected nor received the possibility of split careers – where we went off to learn new skills, or to bear and look after a child, and then returned to the same employer with a warm welcome. Yet in the nineties it isn't just women who have to follow split careers. Everyone with a technical background will require 'retread' times and increasingly they will need to take time out to study other technologies, for it is those with a background understanding of a range of technologies who will have the integrating capacity needed for the future. Education isn't going to stop when we leave university, nor is it going to be possible to acquire new skills in our odd moments of free time, even if we wanted to.

There will always be workaholics in the world, and not only

in Japan, but I doubt that the unhesitating subordination of every other interest, including one's family life, to those of the employer, is going to be the usual pattern. There are other reasons for this. I am writing these words in the midst of a recession, and that is a time when, unless pushed, individuals keep their heads down and sit tight. But in more usual times individuals are much less wedded to the view that they want to work for one firm from school-leaving age until retirement. The actual fact of redundancy itself makes people realise that other worlds do exist and that there are other experiences that they want to explore and enjoy. Increasingly we work not for the bare necessities of life, but for the luxuries. It is, of course, true that a luxury speedily becomes a necessity, but a surprising number of us find it possible to revert to simpler styles of living, and to find different rewards to the single-minded pursuit of wealth and possessions. I am sure that most people need to 'belong' in some way to a group, and those companies which work extensively with outworkers, particularly in the software fields, know the necessity of developing ways of encouraging this feeling. Since I have tried it I am no longer as convinced as I once was that we will all work from home – linked only by an enormous network. I have discovered for myself that working from home means the loss of one's private space and time to a much greater degree than I had envisaged. Even if you operate from a shed at the bottom of the garden you can still pop in to check the fax machine after the first gin and tonic in the evening, or after you get back from the football match on Saturday evening, or whatever. The fact that your work is in your home rapidly erodes the difference between leisure time and work. Moreover, even though it is perfectly easy to keep in contact with other people through the telephone and the fax machine, these contacts are almost bound to be much more closely related to the perceived immediate issues than the general gossip and chat which happens when you meet people face to face. This is not a plea for more gossiping and chatting – but often a great deal more can be gained by informal contact with the people with whom one is working. The contribution which the human mind makes to work and business is very much one of picking up information from tiny, seemingly insignificant trifles, and relating them to new ideas or concepts. I am sure that these are problems which will be overcome and that others, more disciplined than I, will learn how to cope, but at the moment I have found the problems of networking from home much greater than I had expected, while the very thing which I had most cherished and hoped to defend, my home life, has suffered. I am sure however, that the urge for, and tolerance of, difference is already much greater and that managers will have to cater for this.

Organisational conformity and uniformity seem to me to be against the expectations and wishes of employees. People distrust paternalism and have a greatly increased belief in their own capabilities. Practically all the trends that are discernible in individual expectations and aspirations seem to point in the same way. People want more diversity and if it is not forthcoming they will seek it under their own steam. I have friends who have gratefully sought and taken voluntary redundancy or early retirement, because they have wanted to pursue other interests which were not related to the expectations of business. They range from a friend who left to run a steam railway, to another who pursued a lifelong wish to become a butcher. At the same time companies are no longer as demanding of conformity as they used to be – even in the present competitive situation many are recognising that getting the best from people involves giving them 'space' and being tolerant of difference. Unfortunately, this still seems to apply primarily to outstanding individuals who have established a reputation in their own right, such as the outstanding research scientist who has been given immense freedom from enforced rituals of corporate behaviour, in order to encourage his individuality and creativity. I am convinced that this will spread to the stage where individuality is cherished for what it actually is – a sign of the ability to self-start, drive and create, which I am convinced will be the basis for competition in this decade.

I have not attempted to write of the macro-economic changes which represent the inescapable backdrop to all of this. The shift of economic power to the Pacific Basin. The growing concern and awareness of the environmental impact of all that we do (and much that we don't, but should). The problems of a world where we can produce food and products, but have not so far evolved ways in which these can be distributed to the millions in need. All of these factors are the backdrop against which the managers of the nineties will have to play their part. Perhaps the biggest change of all is their conquest of a single world. Changes in communication, the abilities to see things as they happen and the fantastic changes in distribution costs and time. People growing flowers in South East Asia for sale in the markets of Europe, or fresh vegetables in Africa or Australia, for sale in British or American supermarkets. All of these things have already happened and yet in management terms we are hardly beginning to come to terms with their consequences.

I believe that there are more than enough factors at play here to demand a totally different style of management in the nineties. The question is, are we going to have the vision and the creative imagination to develop one? Although the Troubleshooter series has given me an (undeserved) reputation for knowing what should be done, in this case I certainly don't believe I know all the answers. Better answers will be found by younger people than I, the managers who are actually grappling with these changes themselves and will know whether they are the correct ones by the sure test of all managers – whether they succeed or not. In this book, however, I hope to argue that we need to look afresh at how we do things and that new ideas and thinking are both needed and inevitable. If this book succeeds in stimulating some people to look at things in a different way, or to make others more confident that they are treading the correct path, it will have been well worthwhile. The nineties are going to be very different and they will demand a new and different response.

2 Change in the Nineties

Without question, the most desirable management skill for the nineties will be the ability to manage change. This is one of the rarest and most difficult skills to learn – for very good reasons. Management has always been about change, for it is, uniquely, the task of making more, or better, from less. That is, however, a continuum, and is exemplified by the need continuously to improve productivity faster than the competition and, nowadays, by the Japanese determination for continuous incremental development. This sort of change is as much an attitude of mind as it is a specific skill. It is forced upon managers, whether they like it or not, by the need to improve profits and earnings per share every year, and we all know the fate that befalls those of us who fail in this endeavour. The habit of measuring oneself against one's own best achievement is almost second nature to a professional manager. The unwillingness of any board to accept a budget below last year's is a well-recognised fact – often characterised as being unwilling to budget for failure. The pressure for these sort of incremental changes is all-pervasive, and most of us have learnt to accommodate them – albeit with difficulty.

Sadly, incremental change on its own is simply not enough. Indeed, the effort to sustain incremental change all too often obscures the need for bolder, more radical, rearrangement of a whole business, or organisation. In the seventies we were all conversant with the Boston Consulting Group's learning curve theory. Basically this theory was that the cost of a product should be driven down, over time, on what was called a 'learning curve'. The steepness of this line would show whether you were maintaining a competitive lead position or not. The line could go, for example, from ten per cent to thirty, or even forty per cent per annum reduction in costs, when plotted against an adequate time-scale. A flat line was always a sign of imminent trouble. The most interesting use of the learning curve was when a company had been achieving a consistent twenty per cent per annum reduction in costs over a fairly long period, and the line suddenly started to flatten out. Very frequently this was a sign that a major change in technology was overdue. The use of a learning curve was a potent force to drive management towards continuous improvement since, unless it was descending at a consistent rate, it was a sure sign of trouble. Many of us used it as a convenient and well-tried yardstick of what we should be aiming for in terms of cost reduction, or the development of technology. We learnt the hard way that a sure sign of the need for radical change was when the learning curve flattened. It was also a powerful indicator that the technology was about to, or needed to, change. Many research programmes have been initiated because of the realisation that a particular technological approach was nearing the end of its developmental capability.

These facts are only one of the pressures forcing businesses to face up to periodic radical change. Another is the well-observed propensity for organisations to centralise decisions and to grow 'corporate barnacles' on their hulls. These 'barnacles' take the form of organisational programmes and rigidities, which had been introduced, more often than not, to prevent repetitions of mistakes or failures. Such instructions are introduced with increasing rapidity and each new one adds to the rest. Businesses never seem to follow the simple precept of cancelling one instruction for each new one introduced. These coruscations grow – continuously reducing the speed of the hull through the water – until the competition, less encumbered by history and practice, manages to overtake. Chipping away at the growths seldom lightens the load enough. It is actually quicker and easier to do a proper job, and make the big change, than it is to continually fight through the small ones.

Both of these features of corporate life have been with us for a very long time. The frequency of their occurrence has been increasing, but the nature and derivation of the problems remains the same. As I pointed out in Chapter One, however, the nineties will add to these ingrained business patterns by overlaying the whole scene with enormous, and unpredictable, external change. These external changes are occurring simultaneously in the fields of macro-economics, technological and scientific development, and the expectations and aspirations of people all over the world. It is small wonder therefore that, in my belief, the greatest personal skill needed for this decade will be to manage radical change. There is unlikely to be any business or institution which will escape radical change in the nineties and the choices before us are to manage it ourselves or to have such change forced upon us.

Let me speedily disabuse any reader who believes that people can learn to love change. Change means abandoning the predictable and known ways of doing things which we have learnt to adjust to. It means learning new skills, new relationships and new routines with which we are unfamiliar and unconfident. All too often we are required to abandon the safety of the known for only the haziest picture of the future. Nothing is worked out – we are not prepared – and frequently we disbelieve either the need or the solution. It seems as though 'they' are forcing 'their' latest ideas upon us, as they thrash around from unworkable expedient to unworkable expedient. Herein lies the first clue to managing change. It is impossible to change organisations which do not accept the dangers of their present way of doing things. It is certainly true that the greatest risk of all is making no change, because it is inevitable that others will overtake you – but this is a truism that is not always easy to accept. Organisations only change when the people in them change, and people will only change when they accept in their hearts that change must occur. Change is a 'hearts and minds' job and the engines of change are dissatisfaction with, and fear of, maintaining the status quo. It is very difficult indeed to change against the grain of the belief of your people. That grain can be heightened, and indeed must be, but if your people do not accept the imperfections of the present they must be worked on until they do. The fact is that people are more realistic than managers give them credit for. After all, it is they who suffer most from the effects of bad management. They are very aware of the time they waste, away from their main tasks, responding to internal, and often meaningless, instructions and rules. In the overwhelming majority of cases your people are expecting change – and complaining about the lack of it – long before the managers decide to act. For example, in my ICI days everybody knew that the company was substantially over-managed, and that we were not making the best possible speed, given the capability of our people. In practically every pub or bar used by the staff in a large organisation the gossip is almost always about what is wrong, and what could be improved – and people are surprisingly honest with themselves. Obviously there are exceptions – particularly when the need for change is an external one. Your people will know if the order book is falling, the stock building up, the quality unreliable or the customers complaining. They can not be expected to know, unless you tell them, of the threats to the business posed by American or EEC legislation – or the threats posed by the new technology being developed by your competition. It is too late if you wait for the results to show in performance. The need is to make the move the moment the threat is clear and your own vision thought out.

Time spent keeping your people abreast of the changing world is never wasted, but in the nineties it will be critically important. They need to know not only what is going on, but even more, what you intend to do about it – and how you, and they, are going to profit from these events. Your perspective on these matters is a critical part of the creation of an atmosphere which can enable change to occur. If the dissatisfaction is not there it must be created. This is not a quick job. Cosy people do not accept discomfort without a struggle. Continuous examples of the inadequacies of the present are necessary. During my days in sales I noticed that, even though we were still making a nice profit, we were consistently losing sales to one particular competitor. It was all too plain that something was seriously wrong, and I lost no opportunity of pointing out that, plainly, our product could not be as good as we thought it was. It is possible to nag people into a state of mind where they will grudgingly move, rather than endure any more haranguing about their inadequacies, but it is hardly the ideal start for a great crusade. It is better to be patient, and stick firmly to facts which, over a period of time, will speak for themselves. Questions (to which you think you know the answers) like why have we lost customer X, or how does our product match up to competitor Y, help to bring uncomfortable realities into people's minds. Very often a team set up to study why 'they' spend less time making their product than we do, or how 'they' produce so many more winners than we, will act as a catalyst to see the paucity of our emperor's clothes. Each case is different, for each stimulus to change is different, and everyone starts from their own unique launch pad. Nevertheless, it is totally counterproductive to start a change programme unless there is a widespread inner acceptance of the unsatisfactory nature of business as usual.

It is important to recognise two major limitations on managing change. The first, and perhaps most fundamental of all, is that no one 'manages' change – but rather releases and guides it. Management, in most people's eyes, has a pleasing ring of precision, prescience and control. If change is to occur there must be a relaxation on all three of those characteristics. Because change has to be wholeheartedly wished for by everyone, others will inevitably have their own views and convictions on the fastest route to follow. The manager, having released the genie from the bottle, then has two choices. He can try and stuff it back in and start again, with all the consequent loss of energy, time and confidence, or he can try to cajole the released beast in the general direction in which he had hoped to travel. Since it was this particular need which unleashed it in the first place, there is a strong probability going for the manager that this will actually be the route that the genie will choose to take.

The second limitation is the whole question of speed and time. Organisations do not change until the people in those organisations have – and people do not change their ideas and values quickly. Even the best manager's programme for change is very lucky to have achieved its aims in three years – and five years is a more realistic time-scale. Like many things in life, the quicker you get there the less durable the result is likely to be, and five years seems to be about the right period to aim for. Irritatingly enough, there is an upper limit beyond which all is lost. If you find you are still struggling on after seven years you know you've blown it. More than likely you weren't with the grain of your people, and they have grown tired, disillusioned and resistant to your stratagems and pleas. They have long since forgotten where you started from, and could barely care less whither you were heading. The whole process is seen as an irritant, and irrelevant to their contemporary concerns, which are as likely to be about the change process itself as about your business situation or that of the competition.

Given that you have the required dissatisfaction with the present position, the next step is to create a vision of the 'better world' which is going to be sufficiently alluring to tempt us away from today's uncertainties. This vision has to be created by the leader. It has to be his or her dream, but it must, most importantly, be a dream for the business – and more particularly for the people in it. It must not to be too precise, for it has to be owned by others and so it must be capable of the sorts of embellishments and refinements which go with co-ownership, and be qualitative rather than quantitative. No one ever got excited by a dream of growth in earnings per share, but everyone can switch on to being 'the fastest growing something or other'. Everyone can buy in to the idea of being the best in the world, or even at a more prosaic level of being the largest foreign supplier of widgets into Japan. The creation of the vision comprises both a mental target, a long way ahead of where the business wants to be, and an indication of the sort of company that is going to achieve it.

I have watched with growing alarm the spread of mission statements around the corporate world. They almost seem to have been penned by a single great writer in the sky. They are worthy, verbose, exhaustive and exhausting, and are as difficult to attack as the concept of goodness itself. What they don't do is tell anyone what sort of team they want to be. Both for the 'business' vision and the 'people' vision you need a single sentence, without a spare word. The sentences need to aim high, and avoid the 'weasel word' – the word which is used in order to be an acceptable way of presenting the kind of hard truth which we are hesitant to actually express. One company I know describes itself as 'restless and high achieving', another as 'unstuffy and fast moving'. Everyone recognises such words, and those who can operate in such a way will self-select themselves into such firms. When drawing up your vision it is as well to bear in mind just how far ahead you are aiming. Remember that the change plan is a five-year one, so it is not much use setting your sights on where you want to be today. You've got to take a long punt ahead – to the sort of outfit you think you'd like to be in five years' time – even though you won't get it right.

Some things are already clear for the nineties. Does anyone believe the Pacific Rim is not going to go on growing extraordinarily fast? Does anyone really believe that the new Europe will be settled into premature middle age by the mid-nineties? Is it really likely that women will play a lesser role in business life in five years, or that we will all suddenly opt for rigid systems and controls instead of stretch and excitement? I have usually found that the things and ideas which switch me on seem to do the same for others, and that the reverse is also true. People like to work in an exciting and challenging environment, without too much routine, and to feel that they are trusted and treated as partners with similar interests in the success or failure of the enterprise.

Always remember the purpose of the vision. It is the believable, but distant, picture of the place we are heading for, which will be better than where we are today. It is the glimpse of the promised land which makes it worth starting the journey, and it is the obverse of the dissatisfactions with the present which are the other stimuli to start. So it is worth thinking about pretty deeply and, since you will be tested again and again on the depth of your belief and conviction, you'd better believe in it for real.

As well as believing in it, you will be required to communicate it, live by it, and to feel for it with real passion. Without passion and emotion communication is impossible and your vision for your business and its people is quite useless unless others buy into it. You could be forgiven for thinking that once you have achieved dissatisfaction with the status quo, and a shared vision for the future, you would be facing an unstoppable momentum to get on with it, but such is seldom the case.

I said earlier that the engine of change is dissatisfaction but, if that is so, the brake on change is unquestionably fear. Not only is there fear of the unknown – for the vision only covers the ultimate goal, not the long journey to it – but also fear of a more personal kind. Most of us lack confidence in our own abilities – indeed depressingly few of us know or test what those abilities may be. Our normal reaction to a new challenge is conviction that it is beyond us. Even those of us who will 'have a go' do so as much from curiosity, and a determination not to be beaten, as from confidence that we can achieve. In fact it is more often the over-confident who fail, rather than those who doubt their ability to succeed. If these personal fears are not to inhibit us facing up to change we will need a lot of help, and a lot of trust. Above all else we need to know that others have the faith in us that we lack in ourselves. The manager has to instil total belief that he is not asking his people to do things beyond their capabilities, and to demonstrate this continuously. In many cases this will involve training, or retraining, or coaching.

It is not enough to know that you will not be asked to do things the boss wouldn't be capable of doing himself. After all that is why he is the boss. What you need to know is that he will hold you safe from the results of his decisions, and not just chuck you into the deep end of the pool to see whether you sink or swim. You also need to be sure, in your own mind, that if you don't survive you will be treated decently and preserved as an individual. Most change involves losing people. In some cases the change itself is to compensate for taking on and mismanaging too many people for too long. Even when the change involves repositioning a business, it is improbable that everyone will take to the new way of working, or the new skills they are required to learn. No matter how carefully you train and coach there will inevitably be casualties. There are, after all, casualties even in the normal rates of incremental change, and in the nineties we are talking of much more radical matters. The key to looking after people decently, and to taking some of the sting out of leaving the business, is to preserve the individual's self-esteem. This cannot be achieved purely by dishing out money. Money is obviously an essential ingredient in enabling those who leave you to adjust to a new life, but in many ways it is the easiest and cheapest ingredient of all. Inability to cope with change on a personal level inflicts terrible scars on the individual. Sadly, there can be few of us who have not seen friends and their families struggling to re-establish their personal validity after being thoughtlessly and unskilfully dismissed.

In the nineties these experiences are going to be more frequent, unless we learn to do better. The realities of the next decade are that very few of us will go through the period without changing our jobs. There is, however, a great deal of difference between choosing to change your job and believing you have been fired because of your own inadequacy. The awful irony is that it is very seldom that you are fired for your own inadequacy. More often than not you are fired because your managers got it wrong. They either failed to react in time to external threats, or they allowed excessive recruitment, and there is little that you could have done to have avoided your fate. Yet because some stay and you go, you take with you the stigma of failure. Such self-beliefs invariably contain the seeds of their own fulfilment. People who believe themselves inadequate become so, frighteningly quickly, as perceived failure is piled upon perceived failure.

A trail of battered and defeated individuals leaving your company is not going to encourage anyone to change anything. You will never succeed in taking the fear from change. Indeed, in order to keep the adrenalin flowing there must be a sense of urgency, of need and of mission. But you can and must reduce every aspect of the fear which is manageable. Above everything, this is a test of trust – and trust is the most cherished thing that a leader can feel confident about. However, trust is also something that you give, and only if you show your trust and belief in your people will they respond by having trust in you. Cynics, who secretly do not hold their subordinates in high regard, show it in a thousand ways and are rapidly rumbled. They are the first to run around complaining of lack of 'loyalty' and 'trust'. If you are ever tempted to think in these terms I would suggest that you take time out to ask yourself what you have done or not done to create the situation. Remember, management is about leading and change, and if it is to persist it is also about hearts and minds.

Let us assume that, over time, you have got the ground swell going, and have removed the fear. Everyone is more frightened of staying where they are than journeying into the unknown. People believe in the vision and are switched on by it. They trust the management and know that they will be listened to, helped and preserved as individuals either within or without the company. Even when all of this has been achieved, change will not occur without a kick start, together with a few other pre-conditions. One of the key ones should involve a real effort to open up the lines of communication. So much has been written and taught about this that it has become a great big theoretical and practical yawn.

Communications are looked upon as words – and usually written words at that. Written words are notoriously difficult to use as a method of communication, since there are very few of us who can write clearly and concisely. Moreover, written words are seldom personal, although they are often interpreted as such, and the recipient reads them against a background of preconception and belief which the writer seldom comprehends. This is why so many companies waste time and effort in 'memo wars'. Communication in Britain is often about what people don't say, rather than what they do. Uniquely in our country, a manager can interpret his subordinates' silence as assent, while they see it as their ultimate protest. Woe betide the manager who assumes that, just because no one has actually argued with him, his proposal has their support.

The curious thing is that all of us tend to play these games ourselves and yet we often fail to recognise them when we are on the receiving end. The art seems to be perceived as being able to claim that you pointed out the follies ahead, whilst avoiding the unpleasantness of actually doing so in unmistakable terms, and yet it is exactly this sort of obfuscation which leads to trouble ahead. We simply have to learn how to ensure that the points which we are trying to get across are fully understood by the recipient, even if it causes us to test our courage in giving the message. I am often accused of being too blunt in my wish to communicate. However, if you respect others you owe it to them, as well as yourself, to ensure that your viewpoint is really understood. This does not necessarily mean that it has to be accepted. Indeed one of the virtues of bluntness is that you are likely to be told equally uncompromisingly why your ideas are no good. When it comes to major change it is as well to realise that the path you are setting out on is not capable of precise charting. The direction and the approach are, but if change is to occur it cannot be controlled – except on the broadest of fronts. Open communications are the vital lubricant and enabler of this process. But open communications are alien to the culture of most organisations, where responsibility is passed upwards, rather than being felt equally throughout the company.

One of the many hindrances to open communications is internal politics. In turn these are invariably a sign of a badly run, overmanned and overmanaged company. If all your energies are directed at the enemy without (the competition) together with the external links so critical to your success (the suppliers and the customers), there is not much left to divert to internal struggles. In all too many outfits it seems as though a few internal redispositions would put everything right. It is the companies and individuals who are continuously outward looking who will win in the nineties. Politics can be made dangerous to individuals, if challenged head on. 'Business politicians' usually signal their punches a mile ahead, and I think that the best method of dealing with them is to take them directly, on their own ground, rather than trying to out-politic them. A most salutary lesson to anybody who is acting politically in a meeting is to tell him straight out that you believe he is playing politics, rather than doing the job. Everyone knows when someone is speaking politically, or playing political games, and a statement from the chairman, such as, 'Come on Harry, this is far too important an issue for us to waste time while you are playing your political games,' will pre-empt endless plotting and time wasting. Equally the 'bad news' men will have to be encouraged. In an open communications system one should differentiate between the whingers, and the constructive 'no men'. The former, particularly when they whinge after the event that 'they always knew it wouldn't work' are a pain, and should be treated as such. The guys who say, 'this won't work – but this will', are worth a guinea a box, and need to be told so publicly. Even more so when their ideas are taken up and acted upon, as this encourages a behaviour pattern which is vital to change management.

The other preconditions relate to controls and to numbers. Change starts at the top, and by example. The key moving forces are the vision and trust – and trust is exemplified by the cutting of controls. If you examine the procedures that have been built up over time, with the exception of financial controls, most have been allegedly instituted to prevent mistakes. Many have been instituted to limit the responsibilities of those further down the line and to ensure that decisions are delegated upwards. Unfortunately controls seldom do catch mistakes, and in most organisations the problem is to force delegation downwards, rather than suck it upwards. Most people have considerable humility about their own capabilities, and are plagued with self-doubt. They will seek reassurance by asking for advice without being forced to do so. Moreover, their superiors have been promoted due to the excellence with which they did their last job. They feel happier and more effective at supervising the job which led to their promotion than tackling the new and unknown. They are incorrect in this belief, for such is the rate of change that the solutions which worked a year ago seldom work today – but it takes a very good man to recognise this.

Procedures that require sanction from the superior before action is taken have therefore a substantial number of built-in ill-effects. They slow up decision making substantially, they ensure that the decisions are taken away from the centre of the most up-to-date and relevant knowledge, and they reduce the ownership of the problem by the person who actually has to do the job. In addition, as if that were not enough, they provide an escape route for the superior from doing his own job and they also provide substantiative reasons for employing too many people. The commonest complaints about change programmes are that the top and the bottom are OK but the process gets bogged down in the middle. It is always the middle people who are blamed and are believed to be preserving their own entrenched positions and cosy life. This view is the more unfathomable since practically all of us either are in the middle, or have been, or will be. Such is the complexity of organisations, that not only do we actually have lots of people over us, but most of us are blessed with even more who *believe* themselves to be over us, and to have endless rights of interference in our business.

All natural organisational forces lead to more complexity, more centralisation, less delegation and longer and more diffuse chains of command. Endless hierarchical levels are used as a part of the reward system, and promotions, even if almost entirely titular, are seen as the major motivator. Such promotions are used in lieu of praise, reward and recognition of jobs well done, and the withholding of promotion is used instead of reprimands and counselling. Change is almost impossible without tackling many of these issues head on. To a large extent the questions of numbers, organisation, hierarchy and control are intermingled and must be worked on as parts of an interdependent whole. The best place to start is probably with the control systems. The removal of controls leads to dancing in the streets and places responsibility unambiguously where it should actually lie. Secondly it gives a lot of very desirable messages about change and trust, and thirdly the control system, or at least parts of it, is within your own command.

Financial controls are understood and accepted in broad principle by everyone but most levels and methods of application say a lot about the degree of delegation, responsibility and trust. Trying to manage the minutiae from the centre creates work and leads to a secondary industry of control evasion. Nothing will build up the unused stocks of pencils faster than a system which will only issue a new pencil in replacement of an existing stub. The objects of financial controls are to save money across the whole as well as to provide information, and checks and balances, together with some protection against fraud. It is definitely not to save pencils, for it is quite possible that you could save more money by being profligate with pencils and saving the time of expensive people. These are things you, in the centre, cannot know and are arrogant to involve yourself in. Money is saved, speed enhanced, and efficiency increased by passing full financial responsibility as far down the line as possible. Full financial responsibility can only be exercised if information is available in order to exercise it, and it can only work if it is accompanied by freedoms to buy elsewhere, to hire in outside services or staff, to affect the numbers and rewards of the people employed, and so forth. Even then there should be incentives, and recognition of outstanding stewardship. Recognition which takes the form of tightening the forward budgets of the good performers while allowing the poor ones to continue their 'Rake's progress' is not an effective control system, even though it is what happens more often than not. The good performers, as well as being publicly thanked and acknowledged, can, for instance, be encouraged by building up credits to use in the business. The money is invariably well spent, and gives another precious freedom to the individual.

I like to go for substantial financial delegation, and to leave controls in place in the minimum areas of activity. Profits, cash, acquisitions and divestments are the key ones. Sadly, there may need to be controls on capital expenditure but as a rule they are a near total waste of time. In my view it is better to control through cash, than to spend useless hours arguing about the pressure vessels, or the cost of the bicycle shed. The other key controls are certain levels of appointment – but here again clarity is the key. It is necessary to be very clear about who is actually selecting the individual, and who is being consulted. The power to appoint is a key management responsibility and fudging the issue loses a very desirable enhancement of management power.

To some degree the elimination of control systems substantially attacks the bureaucracy which has grown up to administer them. However, bureaucracy seldom withers away without a lot of help. It is not that those enmeshed in these matters either like them or are incapable of enjoying the freedom of headroom and responsibility. People react to the expectations which others have of them and, although everyone complains of overmanagement and obsolete controls, it is extraordinarily difficult to fight free on your own. Over time, a sort of cat's-cradle is devised, so that as one frees oneself from one entanglement, it is only to find oneself in another.

This is why a major change is often easier than chipping away at a succession of minor ones, and why major change has to start at the top. Change is impeded by too many people and too many levels. It only works when the hearts and minds of practically everyone are engaged, and self-evidently this is easier with a few people rather than many. Change involves decentralising, transferring ownership of the problem down to those at the lowest possible level, and continually raising standards and the expectation of results. Above everything organisations cannot change if they are overmanned. 'The Lord finds work for idle hands' and overmanning is synonymous with overmanagement and excessive control. It is also the largest single cause of introspection in companies, which in turn reduces the energy available to attack the competition. The inbuilt tendency in all organisations is for numbers to increase, particularly at the upper levels. It is always easier, and apparently more rewarding and less risky, to make a new and additional promotion, than to push more work further down the line, and take on the task oneself. Eternal vigilance seems to be the only proven method of avoiding this tendency. Therefore, every few years (usually as a result of a downturn in business) we are forced into a demotivating, and often unfair, de-manning exercise. Despite the pain that this produces, both for those who are actually fired, and also for those who have to make the choices and do the firing, we still seem incapable of keeping our organisations lean and happy. This is an area where I would like to think that the nineties will finally teach us the lesson that prevention really is better than cure, but sadly I have not got much confidence that we shall succeed in breaking our behaviour patterns.

Part of the exercise of changing organisations means re-manning to deal with the new objectives and ways of running things. Maintaining controls involves large amounts of time and effort, so obviously cutting them releases people. However, there are two keys to reducing numbers. Little is gained by attempting to 'make people work harder'. Most people have a natural rate of working, which they will maintain in any event. The first key to reducing numbers is to cut out whole areas of activity completely. The second key is to start at the top. People create work for other people, and excess people create extra work. Undermanned organisations are forced to concentrate on the important issues. People simply haven't got the time to waste on non-essentials. The prevention of upward delegation of problems and elimination of controls, supervisory and co-ordinating roles reduces the load on people at the top enormously.

A useful approach to this problem is the concept of 'adding value'. In principle, there should not be a task, role or hierarchical position which does not 'add value' by doing something different to the ones beneath it. The chief executive has unique roles and responsibilities that only he can do. Better by far that he concentrate on these, instead of 'helping' everyone else by doing their jobs as well. If you approach your organisational model by applying these concepts, you will find that layers and levels disappear, almost as if by magic. The numbers needed at the top, for that is where the examination should start, will be rapidly reduced, and the spin-off from that alone is enormous. In the process more responsibility is unequivocally passed down the line – and with it the power and clarity of intent to actively meet the demands which will be put upon the individuals. Reduced layers, reduced numbers, fewer controls and more clarity all produce a virtuous circle which releases energy and increases both the ability to change and the speed with which change can be accomplished.

Many of the ways of doing things in the nineties reinforce one another in this way but few of them can be accomplished without an understanding of the dynamics of change, and what is involved in managing it. If we are successful, by the end of the decade we may have institutionalised the change process, so that it becomes a continuum – instead of a set piece every five to ten years or so. The savings in efficiency, money and, above all, in human pain, will be enormous if we can achieve this. We certainly will not achieve it without changing our own attitudes, skills and management understanding. Change is an attitude of mind and the place to start is within ourselves.

3 Money is the Root of All Evil

Practically all the changes likely to occur in the 1990s are unpredictable and will call for a rapidity of response and flexibility which, even at the best of times, most organisations find difficult – and large centralised organisations almost impossible – to achieve. However, there is at least one fundamental change from the situation to which we became accustomed in the eighties which, in my view, is unlikely to vary – at least until the end of the decade. Money is going to be much less available, and the true cost will be more than we have been accustomed to.

Money is the fuel of the business machine and yet it is extraordinary how feckless many businessmen are in their approach to it. I suspect we have been conditioned by our early experiences. In the bad old days of inflation money was the last thing one wanted. In fact, in high inflation countries the art of business survival is still very much one of not being caught in possession of the stuff, even momentarily! Inflation was the bad manager's friend. Excess stocks apparently appreciated in a miraculous way. The over-capitalised and inefficient investment became, extraordinarily quickly, the cheapest and best plant of its kind. Many of these borrowings were paid back in depreciated currency and there was even a period during which money had a negative real cost – you were almost paid to take it away. Under these circumstances time, as a competitive factor, became pretty well irrelevant, and the prizes went to the large ponderous organisations who could command and deploy substantial resources, no matter how slowly. Levels of decision proliferated, and many a mushroom organisation was built with a massive top, supported on a struggling, over-supervised and under-directed stalk.

Curiously, at this time control of cash was centralised, and looked upon as the finance director's fiefdom. In large organisations cash was a commodity which was hardly mentioned. It was assumed that, as long as total sales revenues exceeded costs, the cash would always be there. Indeed I had worked in industry for many years before I saw a cash flow statement, or a cash flow profile for an investment. This is not to imply that we were totally blind to the importance of stock turnovers and holdings, but these were generally pursued as matters of good practice, with their own measurement systems and targets, and were hardly ever referred to in cash terms.

During the eighties these inflationary effects were largely overcome, to be replaced by a period when banks and financial institutions tumbled over themselves in their anxiety to be first in the queue to lend you money. It was the time when capital seemed to grow on trees, and the only concern seemed to be whether one should borrow more or less. Junk bonds were born, and those with long memories of traumatic times in the past, who safeguarded their gearing, and kept their interest cover high, were looked upon as slow coach fuddy-duddies. They were the tortoises of the business world, who watched the fashionable hares bound past them – apparently to disappear over the horizon to a rosy future.

The hares did indeed disappear over the horizon, but in a very different way from the one which they so confidently envisaged. I am sure that many lenders and investors now wish that they had followed the logic of the change from a high inflation economy through to its conclusion. The recession at the end of the eighties brought these business basics back to mind with a bang. Many a businessman, who had experienced nothing but continuous growth and ready availability of capital, had the difficult experience of learning the art of recessionary management whilst dealing with one. Bad weather sailing is an ability which is best learnt and practised in calm waters, rather than acquired in a hurricane. It is a skill we are all likely to have to exercise much more often in the nineties, and it has its own special rules and practices.

I believe the nineties are going to put a completely new and different emphasis on the management of finance. For a start it seems most improbable that any of us will see a shift away from money being a real cost. If you assume that the real cost of money is the difference between the rate of inflation and the interest rate you pay, the current cost of capital in the United Kingdom is higher than we have been accustomed to for many years.

The art of predicting what these costs are going to be in the future is one that is probably better left to the economists, but my personal view is that it is unlikely that we shall see a return to sustained low real interest rates for some years. This fact alone is enough to sharpen the managerial mind. Practically all companies, when seeking to authorise a new investment, have expectations that a particular rate of return will be achieved. In practice these demands, which are known as the 'hurdle rate', tend to become the aim to which the applicant seeks to aspire – therefore dressing up his request for capital accordingly. All too often these hurdle rates are not, in practice, achieved. Of course the result of all this is that even the few that do achieve their promises are not actually earning an adequate return, because they are not able to compensate for their failed brothers. This is likely to become even more of a problem in the future. Dividends and yields will be in even fiercer competition. Non-earning assets will 'cost' more, in terms of lost opportunities, and the downside of risk investments will be even greater.

However, there is another factor at work which is likely to

have an even greater effect on the ways in which we must manage if we are to succeed. Capital is, and is likely to remain, in short supply, while the need for capital far exceeds our ability to create it. The last decade wasted capital in a whole variety of frightening ways: excessive consumption in the United Kingdom (where did the North Sea Oil revenues go to?); an explosion in credit and borrowing on real estate, houses and land (not only in the UK but in the USA and Japan); massive and ill-judged loans to Third World countries, with high inflation economies, who cannot repay; mind boggling misdirection of capital into military expenditure (in the communist world at the expense of productive investment); the constant flow of money into the pockets of drug barons (little of which found itself rechannelled into productive investment). All of these ill-considered uses of precious assets leave us with a world need for major financial readjustments. The amounts of money required to make good the failure of command economies throughout the world are almost beyond imagination. I know of a service company in Germany which purchased its opposite number in East Germany for a considerable sum of money. So far they have put in a thousand well-trained West German managers to help their Eastern colleagues achieve some sort of comparative competitive effectiveness. In addition, they have already put in one billion Deutschmarks. Remember that this is the commitment of one company, which is servicing an East German population of eighteen million. Multiply that by the numbers of citizens in Eastern Europe, let alone the Soviet Union, and you get some idea of the scale of effort that will be necessary to enable the East to jack themselves up to a profitable competitive position. The Third World, which spent so unwisely on prestige projects and national symbols, like airlines, and high tech plants which they could not operate, have pressing needs of the most basic nature. The problems of the poor in the USA, and the increasing demands of the Japanese for a better quality of life, all bear down on the limited supply of capital the world can generate. In the United Kingdom the problem is not that we have not invested during the last sixty years, but that we have done so so badly. Our school buildings, our roads, our railways, our ports, our services, our capital base in industry, our hospitals, our stock of housing, all show the signs of poor quality investment, which is starting to crumble.

I believe capital will be increasingly difficult to obtain, and that it will be rationed not only by price, but also by the quality and security of the investments we can offer in return. If this view is even partly right, it is going to place new constraints and pressures on managers in businesses of every size. We will have to pay far more attention to the fundamentals of our financial planning. Gone are the days when we decide what we want to do and then, as a secondary consideration, work out how we will finance our dreams.

In reality every business should have more opportunity for investment than finance available. If this is not the case the management are simply not looking at their business clearly. After all, the needs of the shareholders alone can absorb practically any amount of money you have spare. The spectre of businessmen losing sleep because they do not know how to dispose of their surplus cash flow always strikes me as a curious one. Should you really not be able to reinvest productively on the shareholders' behalf you had better return the money to them, so that they can make their own decisions. If this improbable scenario was a rarity in the seventies and eighties, it is definitely a most unlikely one for the nineties. Every one of us will be forced to do our real job, to focus our business ruthlessly back down to its basics, and to concentrate our cash into those areas which we see as representing our advantage over our competitors. Of course we all think we do this already, but the problems of the nineties are going to force us into more and more selectivity. As always in management problems, this process will be complicated by the need to take a long-term view of our businesses, and invest for the future. It is also vital that we maintain the ability to react quickly, which implies carrying excess resources. Both the long-term view and the deliberate carrying of 'surplus' capacity will be higher risk and more costly decisions than in the past. They will demand greater clarity of intention and of the cost/benefits to be expected and will need to be explained and explicit if they are to command the support and patience of the lenders. In turn, lenders are likely to be much more twitchy than in the past, and much quicker to withdraw when they lose confidence. Lenders have incredibly long memories already. Plenty of companies know what a long struggle they have to regain their investors' confidence after there has been a cut in dividends. In the nineties very few managements or companies will get a second chance after a shift in their apparent credit worthiness. It is going to be the lenders' decade, and it is tempting, therefore, to think that the prime management aim should be to avoid risk. To be dull but safe.

From a banker's point of view that would be fine – provided that such policies could generate the earnings to pay off the high cost of borrowing. The reality is that 'dull and safe' will be the most dangerous position that management can adopt. Dull and safe businesses generate dull and safe returns. By definition they are slow to change, and to respond to the fast moving external environment. They will be slow to profit from the technological opportunities which are opening up every day, and they will lose out to their more far sighted, less 'safe' competitors.

These pressures will inevitably heighten the pace and professionalism of management responses and will, I believe, affect every aspect of the way in which we run our businesses. Our financial strategies and visions will have to be an integral part of our thinking at every level of the business. It will be necessary to check continuously how the long-term proposed path for our business measures up against the short-term financial realities. Consistency of vision and aim are thus of even greater importance for our businesses, because they will not be proceeding on a straight and pre-ordained course, but rather tacking their way forward.

When money is tight and expensive the temptation is to centralise and control in more and more detail – itself an expensive and inefficient process. Such a process omits to recognise the key factor at work, which is that expensive money dramatically increases the cost of ponderous and bureaucratic behaviour. Time, as well as being a key source of potential competitive advantage, costs money – and will cost even more in the nineties. The centralised and over-manned organisation will tie up more expensive money in stocks, work in progress, decision time, consultation time, and so on, than its competitor. At the same time such organisations will be losing competitive ground in their ability to meet their customers' needs, bring new products to market, forcing their competitors to react to them, and harnessing the creative capacity of their people.

The paradox which we have to face is that the shortage and expense of capital will put a higher premium on those who succeed in the competitive race while increasing dramatically the handicaps of the losers and the ultimate penalty which they will have to pay. In this environment success can not be easily achieved by the purely financially led company. It will be necessary to manage the business and the finance together as a single whole and it is important to understand that failure of either leg will bring the whole thing down. Under these circumstances it is all too easy for companies to become inward looking and introspective, and to lose sight of the fact that the battleground lies outside. Success goes only to those who satisfy their customers better than the competition does. Apart from wishing to be sure that their suppliers will continue in business, customers are seldom interested in their financial well-being. Customers *are* interested, however, in time. They are interested in quick response, fast delivery, minimum stock levels, minimum cash in the system, innovation, irreproachable and consistent quality – and many less tangible areas of perceived advantage.

Internal financial controls on their own are unlikely to provide this pattern of behaviour. The more so since almost all control systems tend to be broken into very small detailed parts, often without obvious relevance to each other. It is only by looking at the business as a whole, and understanding the broader business and financial goals, that financial performance and customer satisfaction have a chance of being combined. This is a very far cry from the way in which most of our businesses have been run up to now. For a start it involves a great deal of openness. Making financial information available right down the line implies trust – both in the sense of a possible misuse of the information and the risk that harmful facts may flow out of the company to your embarrassment and disadvantage. In my experience, both of these fears are much overplayed. People within the business, even if not in possession of detailed numbers, instinctively know the state of trade – often better than the management. The individuals taking or giving the orders, the delivery men visiting the customers, the machine operator watching the loading – all know you are in trouble – sometimes even before you do. At times of high profit there is also a fear that unreasonable demands for reward will be made. Again, possession of the actual numbers seldom actively makes this process worse. The profitability of the company is in the public domain – it cannot remain a secret, even if this were desirable.

Multiple control systems, which are designed to optimise or control each department's contribution, invariably sub-optimise the whole business and divert attention from the prime needs – which are satisfying the customer and upstaging the competitors. I believe in delegating even areas such as cash controls, as far down the line as possible. Everyone understands cash. In our private lives we all know only too well that if we don't have it we can't spend it – even when it comes to credit cards. Stock turns, work in progress, speed of delivery and order completion all make more sense and immediacy to people if they are expressed in cash terms, rather than in management imposed systems of measurement and control. Delegating cash responsibility can obviate many of the corporate games that are played to make the ratios or the control data look right. Cash flows should still be centralised, so that the finance director can ensure that overnight money is earned, and that cash is earning its keep. Responsibility for collection, minimisation of need, turnaround and so on are all best pushed as far down the line as possible – provided that enough information is also made available for intelligent decisions to be made. I have seen factories operating in a manifestly inefficient manner, largely because of the tightness of the uncoordinated controls exerted on them from above, which have made the achievement of the financial targets much more difficult.

The primary effects of the shortage and cost of capital during the nineties are going to be upon the philosophical ways in which businesses are run. This will bear down very hard on the courage and perceptive capabilities of the management at every level. The effects of these changes will be felt throughout the organisation and will add to the pressures for adaptability and change outlined in the last chapter. The good news is, however, that for once the same reactions are needed to cope with the increasingly financially vigorous climate *and* the requirements to be adaptable and fast changing. The bad news is that these reactions all call for conviction, faith, clarity and calculated risk-taking capacities of a very different order from those which carried us through the eighties.

Even though there are few people who believe that the nineties are going to be easier than the eighties, there are even fewer who recognise the scale of the changes needed. These will put tremendous pressures on managers at every level. Companies will need to trim their numbers, and unless they have a very clear idea of the characteristics that will be required, and how these will differ from those needed in the past, they will stand in considerable danger of losing the very people that they may eventually find will be needed for this new environment. There is always a tendency to keep the 'safe' and reject those who don't fit the mould – to keep those who prospered in yesterday's environment. It is possible, however, that for that very reason these are the people who may find it more difficult to adjust to different circumstances. Ultimately, competitive success depends upon the capabilities and performance of the whole team by comparison with the competition – be it Japanese, American, German or Korean. The prime responsibility of those at the top is to see that the right people, with the right motivation and training, are operating in the right environment for success. There has never been any room for passengers in business. Everyone must contribute if you are to be successful. However, the nature of the nineties will be that it will be even more difficult to carry the 'long stop' type of management. Just as it will be necessary to carry increasing business risks in order to make a profit and survive, so companies will have to take more and more risks on the reliance they place on individuals. On cost grounds alone it will be impossible to carry the plethora of supervision and systems in order to obviate all mistakes. To survive at all, organisations will have to be very tightly manned. Unable to afford the luxury of having multiple cover for every position they will find themselves relying upon the capability and commitment of younger people. Unfortunately, this also has a flip side – which means that it will be necessary to move in quite quickly when it becomes apparent that someone cannot keep up. The luxury of employing someone who makes a significant contribution only occasionally will have to be looked at much more carefully. In this most sensitive of areas time is a luxury one simply cannot afford any more. Holding the balance between speed, tolerance, risk taking, ruthlessness, and preservation of the individual is going to become more critical and more difficult. Very few managers have got this right in the past and it will not get any easier in the future.

It may be helpful to outline some of the main effects which the shortage and cost of capital (and the philosophical changes which derive from it) are likely to have on companies. At the top of the company there will have to be a continual interaction between the strategic goals of the business and the financial strategies which accompany them. In financial terms this will mean that it is important for all the top management to be very clear in their minds about such areas as dividend policy and cover, capital gearing and interest cover, financial market access and acceptability, financial risk profiles, investor profiles, perceptions of the company, and so on. All of these are likely to be quite fluid, for the world of finance is going to have at least as adventurous and bumpy a ride in the nineties as the world of business.

For many years most companies have operated within explicit or implicit financial boundaries, which have been derived, primarily, from established practice and the finance director's views about what would be acceptable to British institutions. In tomorrow's world this approach will not be good enough. The financial markets are already global and they interact with each other with astonishing speed. Nevertheless, such fundamental aspects as the cost of capital and the financing customs of the country concerned differ enormously between, say, Germany, Korea, Japan, and the USA. The nineties will be a period during which many of these differences will be eroded – but even the most dedicated pro-European would be unlikely to forecast a uniform financial system for Europe by the end of the decade. No amount of EEC legislation will open up the Swiss controls on company ownership, or alter the role of equity in the financing of Germany's, largely private, companies.

Companies and managers will have to scan their financial horizons very carefully, as well as those of their customers and competitors. They will probably need to be very aware of national and international trends, for these will have an impact on general expectations, and thus on your access to funding. The availability and location of finance will have a much greater effect on your business aims, so it will therefore be necessary to make a conscious trade-off between the two forms of strategy. It seems likely that, despite the worldwide mobility of capital, some countries, which have different inflationary and balance of payment prospects, will continue to enjoy lower interest costs. Expectations of dividend yields will continue to vary enormously and at present, in the UK, dividend payments are nearly twice the rate of those paid by our German and Japanese competitors. These problems are compounded by the declared expectations of British institutions that dividends should be maintained through thick and (more particularly) thin. The levels of borrowing and gearing which are acceptable to institutions have always varied enormously between countries. Lack of understanding of these differences may well preclude, or hamper, access to markets where capital is more readily available. Despite the sophistication of the way that the markets operate in the whole area of international capital, it seems unlikely that we shall see swift progress to a single unified market in the next few years. History, national preference, vested interests and political factors all tend to hold back our ability to take advantage of the opportunities that modern technology and communications have created for a single, efficient market. If this view is correct, much closer and broader links are needed between business and the financial establishments of the world than those which have usually been maintained by finance directors. In recent years the chairman and chief executive have taken far larger roles in a company's relationships with its investors, and it will be essential that they continue to increase these in the future. The world financial scenario is of such crucial importance that every member of a board of directors must be in a position to interpret its implications for his own areas of business. In turn this also calls for everyone in the company to have much greater clarity about the general financial strategy.

Just as the business strategy must be global for the nineties, so must the financial strategy. Financial considerations will increasingly impinge, not just on the tactics, but on the strategy – and even the business vision. On the face of it many small and medium sized companies may feel that, by limiting growth and ambition, they can escape from all these difficulties. This dream of finding a safe landing place where one can remain – doing familiar, comfortable things and not having to take more and more risks and pressure – is an illusion. Companies which seek to limit their growth and ambition for one reason or another will find themselves facing an unpalatable series of choices. They will probably have to considerably increase the time that it takes to bring new products to their potential market. They will therefore lose their place in the race – finding that the competition is there first. Alternatively, they will find that they are being forced into narrower and narrower niches in order to try to continue to dominate. A policy of continual retreat is not an easy one to manage.

These are the decisions which must be debated and discussed by the top management of the company, and also, since the world is changing so fast and unpredictably, they must be constantly reviewed. They are all things which rely on judgement, and for which there are no clear rules or signposts. Nevertheless, since I believe that the role of management is to take conscious decisions and chart its own specific course, these choices must be faced up to. The basis of the decisions should be very clear, which will thus make it easy to see, at an early stage, when misjudgements have been made and alterations to the plans are needed. This requires openness of mind and a willingness to accept that mistakes have been made. The prizes are won by those who make fewer big mistakes than their competitors and recognise and put them right so quickly that their business momentum is maintained.

Top managers will have to combine an ability to view the whole picture, financial as well as business, with openness of mind, coupled with absolute determination continuously to improve their competitive position. Time must be spent 'tuning in' to world trends, talking to people of varied backgrounds and viewpoints to get an idea of the direction and speed of events. All of these must be viewed against a broad financial backdrop. Because of these complexities leaders of companies will have to accept that they are not the only ones who know best and must harness the widely disparate views of their colleagues. In the past it has been felt that this process was insufficiently positive, and slow. Consensus is viewed as a recipe for indecision and horse-trading in order to reach decisions which are little more than forms of words, rather than recipes for action.

It has to be admitted that consensus has all too often been used in order to run away from the hard decision – but it does not have to be that way. It is ultimately all a question of chairmanship. It is the chairman's job to manage the discussions so that the difficult choices are continuously faced up to and a sense of urgency prevails. This combination of skills and method of working is a rare one and in the past it has not been seen as characteristic of a successful management style. Although these skills lie latent within most of us, it requires careful and conscious tending to bring them out, and to encourage this approach. We have tended to take pride in our mastery of our own patch and to view ourselves as the champions of the perceived interests of that part of the business. This approach costs time, which is better spent stealing a march on the competitors, and also makes it easier to evade the hard choices. Be sure, however, that someone, somewhere, will be facing up to them and that the whole of your operation may well be put at risk through the persistence of pursuing sectarian rather than collegiate interests.

The other vital thing is to learn to delegate and to develop greater trust and openness towards those to whom you have delegated. The only effective way to maximise the generation of cash is to push the responsibility right down the line, but this only works if individuals, as well as having the responsibility, have the power to do something about it. In practically all cases the 'something' they do will probably differ from what you think you would have done in their place. If delegation is to work you simply have to grit your teeth and let them get on with it. The overwhelming balance of probability is that they are right and you are wrong. You are not in possession of as many of the facts as they have, even though you probably feel sure that your greater experience will make up for this minor inconvenience – however, alas, this is wrong. Your experience is out of date. It worked well for you when you did the job years ago, but the world has changed and the nostrum of yesterday simply will not work today. It takes courage and belief to deny yourself the pleasure of intervening, and it is tough to admit that, excellent though you were in your day, it was another day and another world. It takes real guts, once you have forced yourself to keep your sticky fingers out, to accept the responsibility if your protégé fails, while passing the glory on to him if he succeeds.

Similar demands will be made on middle layers of management, where the necessity to take a broad view of the total business will be a completely new requirement for many technically based people. Whilst every manager is accustomed to doing the costing for his own department, and knows his way through the intricacies and loopholes in his part of the management accounting system, it is surprising how little understanding he may have of fiscal accounting.

In many companies the profitability is only known to those at the top, and indeed it is only struck after adding up the totality of production costs and sales revenues. This means to say that, even if the company as a whole wishes to make parts of the outfit further down the line responsible for profit it simply would not be possible, because they do not create the numbers in the right way. Usually financial pressures on a company's performance are best responded to by passing responsibility for profit and cash right down the organisation, but it is unrealistic to do so without providing everyone with an adequate understanding of what is involved. The ability to manage the details of operations on which so much of a firm's effectiveness depends does not marry easily with the ability to take a 'broad brush' view of the totality of the business scene. The man who is a narrow perfectionist in his own field, and one hundred per cent dedicated, can be a dangerous animal in this wider environment. He is likely to be the stumbling block to many collaborative ventures, despite the fact that functional excellence is as necessary now as it was in the past. These attitudes are best inculcated very early on in an industrial career – and they are teachable. However, they will only take root if this questioning approach, where every sacred cow is available for slaughter for the good of the whole, is demonstrated at every level.

The pursuit of both profit and cash does not always proceed in harmony. A very heavy clamp-down on cash availability can force inefficient working and, as well as harming profitability, can actually reduce cash generation. Yet again, clarity of purpose is essential because different external circumstances will produce different priorities. Companies go bankrupt from lack of cash and the first sign of problems are often pressures on cash. The element which links all these things is time and speed. Reduction of cycle time or development time releases cash in a magical way, as well as making capital 'work' more effectively. Not only are these aims contrary to the popular perceptions of the past, but they are also counter-instinctive. It goes against instinct and previous training to carry additional machine capacity in order to substantially reduce the total production cycle-time. All of us have been taught to balance everything, as near as exactly on the head of a pin, but in the process we are actually erecting multiple breaks to slow the whole process up. The idea of running two simultaneous research projects, quite independently of each other, to achieve the same aims would seem completely mad to most business people. And yet this is what the Japanese regularly do – because they believe that the forces of competition between simultaneous programmes will get them there quicker. It is only when you look at the total effect on the business that such techniques as parallel manufacturing, or simultaneous research, or parallel development, begin to make sense.

The shortage and costs of capital will not only make themselves felt in the way that strategy is set out and day-to-day operations are conducted. The shortage of capital will have an immediate and obvious effect on every sort of investment decision. Increasingly we will be looking at new ways of measuring the efficiency with which we use our capital. The pay-back period of investment is something that we will all have to take much more into account, and when we consider investing in new plant and machinery or buying a new business, the very first thing we will look at is the cash generating ability of a new venture. It will be extraordinarily difficult to operate the sort of businesses we have in the past, which have not become cash positive for many years – sometimes even a decade after they started in operation. As far as cash is concerned we will begin to look at cash pay-back periods, as well as investment pay-back periods. Financial stringency places a very high premium on getting it right first time and pre-planning operations, so that everything is to hand and construction time is minimised. The startling speed with which Japanese firms appear to complete projects is not the result of superior rates of working. It is usually achieved by the fact that they have agreed the whole process in detail before construction begins so that it can proceed without continual alteration on the way. Even more to the point, Japanese plants have an irritating habit of actually working when started up whilst, for most of us, the start up is only the beginning of sorting out the bugs in the process.

All these changes create different requirements for management qualities. We have tended to have a high regard for the aggressive 'ramrod' type of manager, who forces action through a reluctant system – the man who fights his corner and brooks no opposition. The qualities we must seek for the nineties are the more controlled and collaborative, forward thinking and creative person; the individual who possesses 'helicopter vision', thinks his way through the opportunities and difficulties ahead and has planned his reaction to them. Moreover, and unusually, he has to be able to visualise the consequences and costs of his actions in a financial sense. The numbers create the scale which in turn will show whether the concept is balanced and viable or not. The understanding of the cash and financial effects will not, in itself, produce a plan for action, or a business concept, but will readily expose the fallacious or impossible dreams for what they are. All management interventions should be of a dynamic nature, inserting themselves into situations which are developing under the dome of external events and the passing of time. The mind that is needed is one that can perceive trends and forecast the range of likely developments. Good managers are seldom taken totally by surprise, for they have thought through the possibilities and alternatives in advance. They are prepared, mentally at least, and often in terms of pre-training and so forth, as well.

The impact of capital shortage will thus have a far more general effect than purely in the financial sphere. It will be even more important to manage the business purposefully, as an integrated whole, and it will sharpen the risks of insufficient action, or ill-considered and excessive action. It will put a premium on flexibility and originality and will provide a bonus to those who can find alternative ways of approaching and achieving their goals. It will change the demands on management at all levels, and will place even greater pressures for change on the largest companies. These companies will, initially, command the easiest access to capital – and yet will find it most difficult to change their managerial and behavioural habits in order to make their capital work effectively.

The pressures for change outlined in the previous chapter will be increased, but they will reward consistency of vision combined with flexibility of tactics. It is those companies whose financial strategy permeates every aspect of their business who will be the ones who reap the rewards.

4 Bad Weather Sailing

In the nineties the abrupt reintroduction to recession and all that it means has been an unwelcome change. Many managers have only known the almost uninterrupted growth of the eighties, and for them the onset of recession has been a totally new experience. For the older ones amongst us it has been an all too familiar return to the business cycles which prevailed whilst we were learning our trade. For most of my managerial life any 'boom' period was spent anxiously scanning the horizon for the 'bust' we knew would follow. The good times were never prolonged enough to sustain the sort of measured expansion and continuous updating of the capital stock which we knew was required if we were to beat the best in the world. However, the flip side was also true. The downturns were abrupt, but they were also short and sharp. On each occasion some companies would go to the wall, but there was always the conviction that the upturn would recur within a relatively short period of time. Within the UK, survival was also helped by low real interest rates and inflation. On balance most of us were more accustomed to bad weather sailing than forging through calm waters. We learnt to keep a sharp lookout for signs of a change and we could swing into a recessionary mode of management almost without effort. The prolonged period of growth from 1982 onwards lulled the senses. By 1989, many managers did not know, or recognise, the early signs to which they should react, so that the recession of 1990 has perhaps proved more painful than it need have done. In addition, many companies had followed the growth philosophies of the eighties and found themselves over-extended on many fronts.

In business terms recessions can be times of opportunity as well as unpleasant experiences and threats. They test the soundness of the management, and mercilessly punish those who are inadequate. They are times when one can gain an advantage against one's local competitors and where your command of your home market can be substantially enhanced. Nevertheless, in international terms it is very difficult to come out in a stronger position *vis-à-vis* competition which has not been coping with a local recessionary environment.

Many management responses to recessionary conditions are not necessarily the expected ones and the right response can really only be learnt as a result of bitter experience or hard analysis and thought. They require the absolute clarity of purpose and willingness to pursue a logical solution through thick and thin, which are the hallmarks of the good manager. The most usual mistakes are slowness, and inadequacy, of reaction. It is as notoriously difficult to catch a deteriorating situation as it is to overtake a competitor who has the initiative. It is only by what may look like overreacting at the first signs of decline that the manager can get ahead of events and remain in control, rather than continuously having to react to the pressures of a worsening situation.

While recessions are times of relative opportunity for those who retain this control and are still working towards their ultimate strategic objectives, these opportunities have a price. One must be prepared to concentrate completely and to abandon all the frills and slightly superfluous activities which have been accumulated in the good times. Recessions are the major slaughtering ground for sacred cows – indeed of any cows at all which do not give milk and can no longer pay their way. It is only by cutting away at everything which is remotely surplus to the main aim that you can hope to maintain your core business intact – and even, hopefully, fitter. It is not surprising that such decisions are shirked, or put off until necessity is proven. One must be prepared to shift, almost overnight, from full ahead to full astern, and yet if you wait until the actions are unavoidable it is almost always too late to keep the core of your business inviolate.

It is vital that you are even more brutally clear as to what the true core business actually is – and whether it is sustainable in cash and financial terms. It is no use trying to hang on to a cash-hungry opportunity in times like these, even if the perceived opportunity dazzles. Survival is the first prerequisite of recessionary management, for without survival there is, self-evidently, no future at all. In these circumstances it is very dangerous to bank on a turn around in any particular time-scale. The bankruptcy courts are littered with people who 'avoided overreacting', and relied on the recession ending by the summer, or the autumn – or whenever. As soon as your nose tells you there is trouble ahead, and well before the order book starts failing, it is vital to get the company into balance. This means cutting away at every possible area, so that costs are covered by minimal revenue earnings. Another familiar trap opens up here. There will be those who genuinely believe that costs cannot be cut further and that, therefore, more expense must be incurred to increase revenue earnings. Very little in business life is totally impossible – but increasing total earnings in a declining market is jolly close to it. People will cling to almost any straw and hope to avoid making cuts. It is amazing how many see their salvation in an expensive advertising campaign, more effort put into selling, a relaunch of the product and so on. All of these actions involve avoidable expense, in the illusory hope that they will more than recoup the outlay. Even in good times there is little direct correlation between expense and return on marketing expenditure of this type. Even when the pay-off occurs, it only does so after a long gap of time, during which the extra expenses are adding to your outgoings. One factor of the recession of the nineties is the impact of high interest rates, which makes the cost of over-extension punitive.

The manager must therefore concentrate on reducing his costs, rather than hoping for an increase in his revenue. If costs genuinely cannot be cut to a level at which cash is not running out, the quicker the business is shut down the better. This conviction alone is often enough to force the realisation that elements of costs which were considered essential are in fact luxuries – and expensive ones at that. Spending money on an extra promotion campaign, hiring more salesmen or elaborate corporate entertaining of customers, merely increases the pain level when cuts have to be made and hastens the approach to disaster. Not only should you not bank on an increase in sales, or a speedy end to recession, it is prudent to assume the worst that you can imagine and then, probably, double it. One of the time hallowed laws of recession is that no matter how bad things are, they can – and probably will – always get worse. No one ever went bust by cutting costs too much. On the contrary, those who get a grip most quickly are those who have the opportunity to buy up the optimists who have hung on in there for too long.

Those who wish to survive, and manage their way through recessions, therefore have to start by concentrating on the control of the outgoings from the business and look anew at every aspect of them. It should go without saying, but seldom does, that such an attack always involves doing things differently. Even an operation run in the sloppiest fashion you can imagine will yield only relatively small savings on telephone bills, stationery and so on. Doing things differently means looking at every major outlay of cash and attacking it with an open mind. One of the aims has to be to transform fixed costs into variable ones. It is surprising how quickly costs build into an inflexible burden which carries on regardless of need or contribution. This trend was given a greater fillip in the sixties and seventies by the prevailing fashion of integrating companies vertically and the belief that companies could provide all their own functions more efficiently themselves. Both of these things inevitably decreased the abilities of companies to react to changes in their downstream activities and increased the pressures on those businesses to keep running for volume, in order that they made a 'contribution'. The eighties revealed the fallacies in these approaches, and the nineties are going to see a further shift away from the old perceived wisdoms. As soon as a service, be it transport, canteens, or computing, is bought in, flexibility is introduced and a part of the total load is shared. Even without the pressures of recession it behoves us all to consider whether we should maintain our own buildings, or own the myriad of specialist services which are necessary for running businesses.

The advantage that a recession brings is, firstly, the concentration of the mind on such matters which, in good times, are viewed as somewhat irrelevant, and secondly, a more general acceptance by people that things cannot go on as they have in the past. Apart from the possibility of relative commercial advantage *vis-à-vis* your competition, this is perhaps the greatest opportunity for business improvement that a time of recession offers. I pointed out earlier the great difficulties of introducing change against the grain of expectation of your people. In bad times everyone knows that change will have to occur. It is not necessary to heighten dissatisfaction with the present. It is more than obvious to every person in the company that the situation is untenable and that change will soon be forced upon you – in the last resort by the company going bust. This part of the change-management process is already done for you and the expectation of your people is not whether, but what, how and when. Surprisingly morale lifts when it is apparent that there is a plan and that nothing is sacred. People are relieved of uncertainty and they channel their energies into actions which they see as relevant to solving the problems. Failure to look at the cost base in this way has exactly the opposite effect. Besides hastening the possible demise of the business, and reducing the room for manoeuvre, there is not enough activity in the company – because of the slump – to occupy the people you have, so that there is plenty of time for them to worry, gossip and play politics. The best of your people will read the writing on the wall and start looking elsewhere. The less good will freeze into a state of inaction and avoid taking any risks. People often seem to believe that keeping their heads down, and avoiding controversy and mistakes, will direct the inevitable sword blows elsewhere. You will find plenty of radical ideas around inside your company, and the more you are able to pick up on and utilise these, the more you will build a feeling of being a team, which also means that there will be more support for the actions which you wish to undertake.

Inevitably there will have to be a reduction in staffing levels, and the way that this is dealt with will have an enormous impact – not only on managing through the recession, but on the whole future of your company. Most managers are only able to take these sort of actions through the conviction that they are saving more than they are losing. It seems blindingly obvious that these situations should be managed in such a way that as few of your people as possible are worried, frightened and concerned about their future. During these times it is vital that your core business, and key people, are powering onwards in order to gain the maximum advantage against your competitors. It is unlikely that your troops will give of their best if they spend most of their time scanning the situations vacant adverts and preparing their families for the worst. Unless it is a really badly run company, however, those at risk will probably only be a minority, and very few of those through any fault of their own. Surely these people deserve the consideration of being given the maximum warning, so that they can do a little forward planning for their uncertain futures. In most companies about ten per cent of your employees are almost certain to have to go, and probably another twenty per cent are at risk. Over half of all your people have as much security as anyone in business ever has and they should not be distracted from working for the future of the company, and for themselves and their colleagues. Dealing with people in a straightforward manner in this situation is often shirked and every sort of plausible reason is produced as to why nothing should be said to anyone until everything has been worked out. The result of this is to have all of your employees worried and concerned. It is better by far to direct the energies of those at risk to their own futures, whilst ensuring that the remainder keep their eyes on the ball – for there is more than enough for everyone to do, if you are all to come out of things for the best. The way in which you deal with your casualties will have a big effect, not only on them and their families, but also on those who remain. Moreover, the business situation is a dynamic one and the future is never going to be predictable enough for you to give your people absolute assurance – in today's climate no company or organisation is strong enough to be able to guarantee security of employment.

Having said this, I do believe that every company and organisation can, and should, guarantee involvement and concern with their employees' futures – either within or without their direct employment. This involvement can take many forms. It signifies a determination to prepare individuals properly, so that they can face the future demands upon them. Within the company, that means a commitment to training people for the new demands and responsibilities that they will have to face. It means genuinely trying to help the people who have to leave to find the career and lifestyle best suited to them for the future. It can pay handsomely to try to help your people into whichever new job or career they want to follow. In many cases retraining in a new skill can open new opportunities. It is surprising how many people have found fulfilment after the apparent disaster of redundancy. When you lose your job it is very difficult to look upon it as a new opportunity, and almost impossible to do so without help and support. People need time to adjust, and need help with their feelings of loneliness and abandonment. Even companies which avoid paternalism still provide a background of some security and companionship, which are the more marked when they are no longer available.

It can be mutually advantageous to look at setting up your own people as independent suppliers of the services which they have performed for you. They can then seek other outlets for their services and you can concentrate on the business which is your main aim. Flexibility is introduced for both of you. People think in terms of management buy-outs in this context, but the same technique can work on a far less grandiose scale. Your groundsmen and gardeners, your cleaners or canteens can all be self-standing businesses in their own right. Individuals, as well as groups of people, need a 'fairy godmother' to help them in their transitions, and often a little help or advice on financing, accounting, selling or pricing are less costly to you, and more valuable to the recipients, than the application of pure money. Of course money is needed, but on its own it seldom meets the objective. It is vital that your people retain their self-respect, and remember your company as a decent employer. Nothing lasts forever, and when the recession is over, and you are trying to attract the brightest and best away from your competitors, your reputation will be a key factor. Few companies can succeed in the long haul if those who leave them spend their time spreading the bad word. Moreover, closer to home, those who remain, whom you are relying upon, will keep in touch with their friends and colleagues who have moved on. If they see a trail of broken families and prematurely ageing individuals, who have lost the will to fight, they may value their job

– but will they take the risk and own the problems your company is facing?

In this difficult area of reducing numbers, as in everything else in recessionary management, selectivity and focus is the absolute key. If you are to lose ten or fifteen per cent of your people you should do everything possible to ensure that, from your point of view, they are the right ones. Remember, when selecting people for the future, the demands on them will be different to those of the past. It is always important to look at people's track record of achievement, rather than the cosiness of their behaviour. In a business sense very little can be achieved by individuals on their own. It is often very difficult to work out who, in reality, has actually been the prime mover for success. Everyone wants to claim the successes, while few people are prepared to own up to the failures. Success is, in any event, a relative rather than an absolute thing. A man put in to turn around a business, who instead sells it off or shuts it down, may actually have achieved a success. Reducing the rate of loss in a 'lost cause' business may be a success, whilst failing to grow a successful one at its fastest possible rate may be failure. The people you want in your team for the future are those who have a continuous track record of being in businesses that have changed and improved and have always been ambitious in their aims. You want people who can work with others. Some people are the human equivalent of catalysts. Their involvement is crucial in terms of creating change within the team and a new freshness of approach and attack. You need people who will forgo apparent personal advantage for the sake of the group as a whole, and people with originality of view, who are their own men. Inevitably these individuals cause waves and are not always valued when the going is easy. The temptation is to let them go (and they will be more than ready to do so) and keep the 'reliable' team men, who will always agree. The difficulty with this approach is that you are losing the prime movers, and the problems in recession are to move faster and more purposefully than your less hard driving and single-minded competitors. Time spent thinking through this situation is never wasted and it is an area where individuals' differences of view, and of capabilities and contributions, are very valuable. Very often one of your colleagues may have seen Mr X in a different situation, or a different light. It is notoriously difficult to backtrack if you make a mistake. Re-hiring the person you have made redundant is as difficult for him as it is for you – so you had better make sure you get it right first time.

Recessions are key times for training and, for the first time in my experience, many companies seem to have continued training their people through this downturn. Most people view this as a sign of confidence and it is very reassuring for those whom you wish to keep. The one big downside of training that companies often cite is that while their people are being trained they are not actively making money for them. However, it does enable you to enhance your competitive advantage when the upturn comes, and – have confidence – it eventually will.

The next area to address is the whole field of your assets and their contribution to your business goal. Even when you have identified the activities that are not contributing now, and are not vital for the future, there is the greatest reluctance to dispose of them. The argument, and it is a siren song, is that when the recession is over you will get a much greater price for whatever asset is under discussion. It is a tempting thought, but it is wrong. During recession money in the bank is the key to success. Those who have it can buy bargains they have never dreamt of. Realism alone should press you to turn every non-earning asset you can into cash as quickly as possible, and reinvest only into the key areas for your future. Pride, and fear of what other people will think, often prevents companies taking such action. The worry is that your creditors, competitors and customers will all assume the worst when they see you selling and leasing back your headquarters, or shutting down the company flat or entertaining facilities. Even if such reactions do initially occur it is surprising how quickly these attitudes will change when you are seen to be strengthening your balance sheet and to be the proud possessor of liquidity.

Few businessmen in the UK need telling that recessions are times when the happy relationship which you have hitherto enjoyed with your banker undergoes a surprising change. Debt, which after all is the business of banks, seems to have a very different ring when times are bad. Banks and creditors get very twitchy and are prone to place inhibitions and restraints on freedom of action. Creditors will not often move in this way whilst they can see managers operating in a determined way against non-performing assets. In good times holding large, positive cash balances can invite predators. Nothing can be so infuriating as a hostile bid which has been attracted by the notion of buying you with your own money. Stock markets tend to take a kinder view of unutilised cash balances during recessionary times, and shareholders are markedly less enthusiastic about trading your cash for some-one else's paper. In good times companies are criticised for holding cash and it is assumed that they can find no worth-while internal investment for it. These criticisms are also lulled in recessionary times. Self-discipline and strength of purpose are heavily tested if you are to avoid the temptation to take a flier and spend your new-found wealth at the first opportunity. For those who bide their time and are clear about their business aims, however, the advantages are overwhelming.

It is not only in the area of asset sales that this emphasis on cash is so critical. Companies that go to the wall during recessionary times do so because they run out of cash. Companies can survive for a very long time without profit – but cash shortage is self-accelerating and hits with the speed and destructive force of a typhoon. In the previous chapter I wrote about the subject of cash management and my views on how this can be maximised in the normal running of a business. In a recession, however, this aspect of management must be emphasised above all other considerations except the overriding need for focus. Even when looking at the core business, its cash characteristics and sustainability during bad times are a key consideration. The same concerns with cash inevitably impinge on capital investment. It is essential to keep on investing in the core business, but everywhere else only proposals with the shortest possible pay-back should get through. This is hard to achieve, for the prices of equipment and the cost of projects fall to undreamt of levels, but such temptations must be ignored in the sacred name of concentration. Money must only be spent on very quick, risk-free, increases in profitability. This means eschewing expansion and concentrating again on the cost side of things, and this only where letting out work to others cannot achieve a similar result.

This same level of concentration should also be directed at your customers. Here again the action required is counter intuitive. In good times it is always tempting to heave a sigh of relief when an 'awkward' customer takes his business elsewhere – the kind of 'awkward' customer who is continually on the phone chasing up any minor lapse in quality or delivery, the man who queries the price rise that others have accepted. So much easier in such circumstances to stay with the type of customer who never rocks the boat and never seems to notice your failings. The snag is that in hard times this is precisely the sort of business that may not survive. It is the 'awkward squad', who run a tight ship, who are the ones who will survive and will probably emerge even stronger. In the recession it is exactly these 'awkward' customers with whom you should be building your relationships. It is as well to take a good look over your customer base and try to decide which ones are likely to be the long-term players. It is even more important to do so if you are not a supplier to the strongest player. Your business is only as good as your customer base. It is not much use assuming that one hundred per cent of Lada is equivalent to five per cent of Mercedes. The tough customer gives you much more than survival. He sets the standards and it is he who is moving ahead – and with luck he will be carrying you along in his wake.

All of this does not mean that you should just abandon your old relaxed and uncomplaining customer. A bit of constructive help to improve things such as his consistency of delivery may actually assist both of you. Recessionary times are ones, sadly, in which the old adversarial relationship between customers and suppliers can so easily take over. The belief that it is a good idea to force your supplier into making things for you at a loss seems to triumph over a more rational longer term view. Recessions are times when, in your own self-interest, misery should be shared and sensible businessmen build the relationships which, alone, will give them the chance to optimise the effectiveness of the ways in which they work. There is far more cash to be shaken out of the system by working together than by trying to make your position better at someone else's expense.

Despite the fact that cash in the hand is so important, one of the most unhelpful and yet widely practised methods of all is to delay payments to suppliers, either overtly or by continuous bureaucratic filibustering. Leaving aside the fact that I believe it to be immoral to renege deliberately on a freely entered contract, it is also self-defeating. The habit swiftly spreads to your own customers and the end result is a classic game of 'beggar my neighbour'. After all, hopefully, you aim to sell more than you buy, so even self-interest should persuade you to observe the agreed terms of business scrupulously. It is surprising how often 'misery sharing' actually eases the misery. Working together to reduce costs rather than 'passing the parcel' is not only more constructive but it actually works.

I know of more than one large group of companies who, unable to accept price increases from their suppliers, offered instead to put their own people in, in order to help improve efficiency, and then shared the resultant economies. Forcing your established suppliers out of business usually increases your costs in the short term, even if you can persuade yourself that you have gained in the long run.

The next area to address is the whole one of internal communications. Recessions are times of rumour. Even the best informed and most open of companies are prone to flights of internal fantasy which can make *Alice in Wonderland* look factual. No idea, theory or ill-informed addition of two and two to make twenty-two, is too far-fetched to spread, and they all engender alarm and despondency. After all, people are frightened. They are surrounded by bad news; factory closures, company bankruptcies, redundancies, people's marriages collapsing, youngsters being returned from school, houses being repossessed – small wonder, therefore, in the absence of trust and freely available internal information, that fantasy and fear take hold. Managers' usual reaction in times of uncertainty is to become more secretive. They do not want to reveal their own lack of certainty and they fear that if they have to retract statements which they made in good faith, they will lose their shaky command of the situation. The truth is the reverse. The conviction that news will not be withheld – be it good or bad – helps to build trust and confidence. The irony is that, no matter how bad the news, it will almost always be less bad than your people are expecting. In bad times there should be no surprises in a well-managed business. The facts of the business situation will speak for themselves if they are openly shared, and the knowledge that the management are fighting hard for the business is what builds the team spirit. Even if you are sure that you have thought of every contingency or possibility, there is almost bound to be someone, somewhere in your outfit, who will have thought of something else that can be tried. In hard times companies where everyone knows what they are aiming for, and believes their help and involvement to be of critical importance if the company is to succeed, have a very different feeling to others. Sadly, we have all seen businesses under pressure where everyone is blaming everyone else. A sort of paralysis of inaction sets in, which inevitably produces tragic consequences.

It is no use doing all the difficult things which I have described unless people know what is being done and why. Indeed unless they do, it is unlikely that the actions will actually be carried out or followed through. People do not expect their bosses to be omniscient and they understand the uncertainties of the future and the ease with which a business can lose command of its own destiny. They do expect, however, that at any particular moment their boss will know what he wants done, and why. As long as they know why they will forgive a change of direction when something does not work, or the external situation changes.

Since only a united team is likely to prosper in bad times it makes sense to treat every one of them as a fully paid up member – for they are. It is not just your job, the shareholders' money and the company's future that is at stake – it is their lives and futures as well. They are entitled to know, and the rewards of informing them properly, continually and bluntly, far outweigh the small risk engendered by so doing.

To summarise, therefore, bad weather sailing is very different from good weather cruising and many of the required actions are not the expected ones. It is essential to retain the managerial initiative, for your aim must be to come out at the end in a stronger position than your natural competitors. This is particularly vital when you consider that those in countries not undergoing recession will have been sailing happily on whilst you have been manning the pumps.

The keys to recessionary management are the four 'Cs':

concentration, costs, cash and communication. Every action taken must be selective, and designed to strengthen your core business. The first requirement is clarity of focus about where you wish to end up, followed by a savage and calculated attack on costs. Remember that cash is the key to success. Assets must be ruthlessly disposed of, even at apparently sacrificial prices, if you are to have the financial headroom which will enable you to take advantage of the bargains which will inevitably appear.

Care for your people. Help those who have to leave you to retain their self-esteem. Reassure and train those whom you wish to keep for the next march forward. Treat everyone as you would want to be treated yourself – that means different, and personal, treatment of every individual. Communicate relentlessly. Far better to bore people with over-communication than to terrify them by allowing rumour to fill the vacuum.

If you do all of these things you will build a solid team and ensure that you have a really powerful and committed base for the good times ahead.

5 Over the Water

Any businessmen would have to be blind as well as deaf to be unaware that 1993 was the alleged birth date of the single market. For the last five years we have been alerted, cajoled, threatened and enticed towards this mystical event – scheduled for the 1st January 1993. All the more surprising, therefore, that so many of us are still unaware of, and unprepared for, the impact which this will inevitably have on every business – no matter how small or isolated.

Moreover, for a number of clear reasons, we are temperamentally and historically less well prepared for this event than our continental competitors. By virtue of their geographical location practically all continental businesses have to serve other national markets besides their own. It is very difficult for a company in Holland, Belgium, Switzerland or Denmark to exist on their home markets alone. If you are located in the Vorarlberg you tend to look equally naturally to Germany, Austria and Switzerland. If you are in Holland you think of Benelux and Northern Germany as readily as we do of Yorkshire or Devonshire. The concept of trading across frontiers, of being exposed to competition from other nations, of having to cope with differing standards, exchange rates and laws is a natural part of your everyday life. This is not the case for most of us in Britain. Selling to a customer on the mainland of Europe is still counted as an export, and an adventure, despite the fact that it may very well be easier and cheaper to deal with a customer there than to do the same for someone in Dumfries.

Looking at it from the other point of view, companies based in mainland Europe feel quite relaxed about relying on continental suppliers, whilst they are often quite anxious about the reliability of supply if they are purchasing from a company in the UK. Even today, when cross-channel delivery has not been interrupted for more than ten years, and only the dockers can remember the last dock strike, it is by no means unusual for British companies to be expected to hold a local stock, as a condition to becoming a supplier to a continental manufacturer. Perhaps these are some of the reasons why so many British businessmen and women tend to view the single market as a threat. Our European competitors, however, see juicy pickings in Britain and do not appear to be worried about the prospect of our own onslaught on their home ground. After all, they have learnt how to cope with interlopers of other nationalities over a great many years, and why should they fear the British any more than the Italians, Germans or French?

To plan adequately for the future of our businesses we have to look a good deal further ahead, at some of the fundamental changes which are occurring. Then we must ask ourselves how these changes affect us, and how we can turn them to our advantage. There is much more to this than just bracing ourselves for a more competitive environment – even though the environment *is* indeed certain to be a more competitive one! The prizes will go to those who have methodically set out their stall in order to be successful survivors in the next century. The processes of change which are underway will make the problems of recessionary management look like a clam bake. There are no blueprints or models for the restructuring of an entire continent's industrial structure in such a short period of time. The only example one can look at is the USA and the way that business patterns there have evolved

over nearly a century of progressive change – and even that is
not a parallel.

Let us look at some of the fundamental differences. Even
though the law of comparative economic advantage is slowly
working through in Europe, it has been delayed, hindered
and hampered for nationalistic reasons. As a broad generalisation our industrial map has grown on a national basis. Every
country has, in order to preserve internal competition, sought
to have at least two manufacturers or businesses of every kind.
Where the forces for external competition have threatened,
say the French car industry, or German aerospace, governments have moved in swiftly to try to turn back the tide. The
result of all this has been a startling fragmentation of the
market. Even though the EEC population of 350 million is
larger than the USA's 290 million, the disparity in the number
of companies sharing each of these markets is very striking.
Typically, in the USA, eighty per cent of the market is
covered by a probable maximum of five main players. The
market leader in the US will have a twenty to thirty per cent
share of the market and will use the power of that position to
establish a degree of price and quality leadership. The same
market in Europe will see a similar eighty per cent shared, not
infrequently, by twenty or more players – and the market
leader has performed prodigies if he commands ten per cent
of the whole.

It is not just the richness of our cultural and historical
diversity that demands endless varieties of a product. None of
the many standards are common ones, something which is
probably not helped by this national fragmentation. In world
competitive terms this is a recipe for high costs and ineffi-
ciency. I am no believer that big is best, but, where Toyota
produces more cars than Mercedes, BMW and VW combined,
it is not easy for these splendid standard bearers of quality
and design to stay ahead. It is very difficult for them to fund
the new development and new products, on a comparative

level, which are the only things which will enable them to beat what is coming at them. Size does not guarantee success, for all too often size equates with slowness and stodginess, but size, accompanied by demanding, ambitious management – busting a gut to be the world champion – will always take a lot of beating. The single market is aimed at attacking the historical barriers which have hindered the emergence of clear European champions. It is aimed at producing an environment which encourages the most efficient, effective way of serving our 350 million customers, an environment which will help our businesses to gain the world competitive advantage which such a home market should give them.

This implies a period of continuous and experimental restructuring of our historically derived industrial and business base, the removal of European Tonnes of overhead and the refocusing of our businesses into dominating groupings in niches of the market – be they large or small. Because we have no supra-national Government – no matter what the gloom mongers may say – this process of restructuring will be market driven. It will occur because of economic forces – but it will be fashioned by the dreams and vision of the businessmen of Europe. The question is, therefore, do we want to lead the restructuring – or are we content to be one of the restructured, disappearing before the inevitable pressures of those who are driving ahead? It is, I believe, a mistake to push historical analogy too far. Restructuring does not necessarily mean 1900-type domination by monolithic pan-European companies. It can, and will, take a wide variety of different forms, alliances, networks, co-operative shareholdings and some concentration into single ownership groups. The process is, I believe, inevitable and the prizes will go to those who recognise and utilise this process, and use it to ensure the growth of their business.

Woe betide the company which believes itself to be immune to the impact of global and European competition. The decline in the number of fish and chip shops in the UK from 40,000 to

9,000 is eloquent testimony to the international nature of competition. This reflects not only the competition from fast food outlets such as McDonalds, but also the growing interest in Chinese and Indian takeaways and other 'exotic' convenience foods. In another area, I know of some provincial lawyers and estate agents who have recognised similar trends at an early stage and have actively sought ways to broaden their business into this enlarged and challenging market. Even if you do not feel competition directly from Europe you are bound to be hit by one of the resultant business reverberations.

In all of these changes, as always, attack is the best form of defence. It is far less effective to react to the probing and pushing of someone into your marketplace, than to force him to react to your ingress into his. The first essential in all of this is a determined attempt to broaden your knowledge of what is going on, and to spend some time and effort to understand the variations and complexities of the different markets you are aiming at. It is a great mistake to assume that a single market means uniformity of taste and business practice. It is a happy chance that British black pudding makers can compete and win the French championships. The product and concept is very different in Germany or Greece. It has always been a surprise to me that the USA, with its vast range of geographic, climatic and cultural diversity, has had so many products that sell across the country. Nevertheless, the sales of Texan ten-gallon hats in Alaska are, I guess, as circumscribed as the sales of sleigh-dog harnesses in Houston. The ubiquity of many American products and brands owes as much to a combination of a single language, education system, networked television and press coverage and the spread of retail chains throughout the Union, as it does to the legal and commercial singularity of the country. Until recently the USA has been a cultural melting pot. Even the most ardent Europhile finds it hard to imagine Europe following America's path in this. The strengths of our continent lie in its differences of taste, design, habits and preference. One of the most difficult decisions facing a businessman is whether to adapt a product to meet these differences, or whether the demand for the product is strong enough for it to sell in its own right. Even though any European traveller knows the tremendous variance in chocolates between countries, products such as KitKat bars, Mars bars and Belgian chocolates transcend frontiers. On the other hand, one would have thought of Europe as an ideal marketplace for the evolution of a single type of washing machine – but inspection reveals that the British prefer front loaders, the French top loaders, the Germans fast spin driers and the Italians slow spin driers. For commercial success, these preferences should be respected. Today's manufacturer can relatively easily produce all these variants in a single factory. Thought and planning put into that process will probably be much more rewarding than trying to sell machines against the preference of customers.

Chambers of Commerce, Trade Associations, Consultants, the Foreign Office, the BOTC, the EEC and market research firms, as well as business information companies such as the Economist Intelligence Unit, can all produce the background information you need in order to assess the market opportunity awaiting you. There is, however, no substitute for a businessman's version of the 'Grand Tour' and going to look for oneself. Once you have reconnoitred, a whole range of bewildering choices has to be made. Are you going to 'export' from your existing plants, are you going to buy a continental competitor and build on his presence, are you going to 'greenfield' it, or are you going to try, initially at any rate, to form a loose alliance? There is so much to learn, and so much change taking place, that there is quite a lot to be said for small and medium sized companies settling for an alliance. This is relatively low risk, and low exposure in financial terms, but difficult in human and emotional terms.

The 'chemistry' of the relationship is of central importance if you are going to follow this route. No matter how much the courtship seems to have been selected in heaven, like all courtships it will have its rough moments and may well test your resolve cruelly. The EEC run a sort of business 'dating agency' which will put you in touch with business people in other countries who are seeking to form alliances with British companies. At the very least, this can give you some calling points on your 'Grand Tour'.

No matter how wide ranging your ultimate ambitions are, it is wise to limit yourself to gaining experience of one new country and company at a time. I know of two attempts to form a triple (and in one case a quadruple) alliance in one mighty bound, and in both cases there have been problems. The difficulties of building up trust, confidence and an easy working relationship, are not double or triple but squared and increased by the power of three. There is a natural rate at which organisations of different national origins can learn to work together and it is wise to accept this. Attempts to compress the process introduce strains of their own and seldom succeed. It really is a case of more haste less speed, and it is better to have covered two countries soundly than to have allies in four different countries which are unable to find satisfactory ways of working together.

Whether you decide to go it alone, or in partnership, it is sensible to look at the single market from a completely new perspective. The locations of many plants, headquarters, offices etc have been selected because of historic limitations. Many manufacturers sought political advantage by locating a factory in each country which they sought to serve. Many others located in countries in order to serve industries which are no longer there. One of the immediate effects of the single market legislation should be a striking reduction in distribution costs. The removal of cabotage alone will have a dramatic effect, and the competitive pressures of the Channel tunnel on

North Sea ferry rates are already clear. Distribution costs are usually looked at most carefully when one is first investing, but as time passes are seldom watched as keenly by top management as they should be. It is as well to take a careful look at the European map. It is important to look, not only at where demand is at the present moment, but also at where you believe the future growth for your product or services will be the fastest. The demographic trends in the countries of Europe could hardly differ more dramatically. Unexpectedly, yesterday's baby-boomers seem set fair to be tomorrow's one-child families. The companies which I believe stand the best chance are those which are prepared radically to redesign and refashion their businesses in order to address tomorrow's opportunities. This means having a view of where your market will be served from in ten or twenty years' time, rather than thinking of it in terms of two or three years ahead. This is an area where the businessman who gets out and about – who is constantly looking at the world from different viewpoints and sharing his perceptions with his colleagues at all levels in his firm – can gain a real advantage over his competitors. Very frequently it is people who are really close to the market, such as the representatives or the buying department, who can see the way that trends are moving. However, if you are trying to take a very long view you have to consider the basic situation and apply it to your own perceptions and beliefs about the direction that history is taking us. It is already, for example, fairly obvious that at some time in the next century the old 'Eastern Bloc' will be one of the most competitive parts of the world. Just as Germany was totally re-equipped after the last war, so they will have a brand new capital base in every area, be it telecommunications, railway systems, roads or whatever. In addition, their factories will be the most modern and, because they are having to learn skills from scratch, they will be amongst the most open thinking in the world. The problems with trying to look ahead in this way are that we know that the future is not an extrapolation of the past. Demographic trends are already there for everyone to see, and can only change over a period of time, as can education and other systems. But the actual combinations of all these things are subject to different processes and pressures, and it is the ability to look at the fundamentals and to apply creative imagination to the probable trends which will enable business people to prepare for the future. Even if you start now it will be quite a race to realign within seven years – and what could be worse than to put all that effort into producing the ideal set-up to serve yesterday's demand?

Even with all the new legislation, it will take time for working processes to develop. It is only in the last two years that we have seen hostile takeover bids in Germany and only very recently that we have seen the highly protective ownership structures of Swiss companies beginning to open up. Even if a 'level playing field' were possible it will take a lot more than level legislation to effect it. It is also foolish to assume that one can pre-judge the actual form of this playing field – or even of the game which will be played upon it. Because in the UK we have one of the highest rates of enacting EEC legislation into national law, we are particularly prone to assume that an EEC *diktat* is equivalent to a single-market law. In fact it only becomes so when each country has concluded their own internal legislation, which can often take a very long time. National legislatures have found plenty of reasons for delay, and some have developed high levels of skill at ameliorating the effects of EEC directives which they see as inimical to their national interests. In Britain we tend to think of the French and the Italians as past masters of this game – but they are by no means alone, and Germany is not always the upright supporter of the single market that we give it credit for.

To add to all these complexities, those of us who are trying to chart our way into the future now have to spread our tarot cards even further. The freeing of the Eastern Bloc introduces totally new dimensions to all our forward thinking. I am not one of those who see Eastern Europe as an area of limitless immediate opportunity. One of the immutable (to say nothing of obvious) laws of business is that it is very difficult to make money out of people who do not have any. However if we look ahead, the collapse of communism gives European business long-haul strategic opportunities beyond our wildest dreams. Few would now argue that the Marshall Plan harmed American economic growth in the years after its generous introduction. Indeed the transformation of Europe from its war-torn wreckage provided an added stimulus to American economic power in the intermediate term. Much of my early business life was bound by a fanciful picture of American business and financial domination of Europe, and by the clear conviction that the American economy was, and would remain, all powerful.

It does not take an enormous leap of imagination to think that in thirty years or so Eastern Europe could be the source of growth and economic dominance. Over the next few years they will build a totally new infrastructure. They will probably have the most modern telecommunications systems in the world and many of the newest and best equipped factories. Their people have a pressing need for success, both personal and economic. They are well trained, albeit narrowly, and have every incentive to make things happen as fast as possible. These changes should present medium-term, as well as long-term, opportunities or threats.

If you agree with this view, or even consider it a long odds runner, it is worth thinking now about what you are going to do about it. Eastern Europeans have long memories, and those who become involved in a practical way, early on, are likely to be the ones who reap the rewards in the future. However a great deal of effort will be wasted, and relationships may well be permanently damaged, if you start something which you are unable to keep going in the long term. You should be aware that an Eastern European's idea of 'long term' is much longer than ours, and you will probably be looking at ten years or more. With the present and likely continuing cost of money there are very few companies who can afford so long a pay-back period, and therein lies the rub. There is very little to actually buy in Eastern Europe. Because they have worked in a command economy, there is no such thing as a market position, as we would recognise it. Distribution, dealer networks, maintenance facilities and branding are all conspicuous by their absence. Manufacturing facilities are all too often hopelessly out of date and poorly maintained. At the glass company which I visited in Poland they were really unable to get their minds around the costs of carrying stock. Although they were aware that cash actually cost money, they still failed to realise the enormous costs of carrying the stock which was piling up around them and were therefore unwilling to consider stopping making the product. They were deeply concerned about the costs of starting up the line once it had shut down – which they knew with great accuracy – but they simply missed the other part of the sum, because it was not something for which they had been held responsible in the past. Similarly, the workers had been trained in manual skills and understood the demands of keeping a very old-fashioned production line running, but would have been completely incapable of coping with computer controlled machinery. There is nothing the matter with the potential of the Polish workers, but time is not on their side and moving into line with the West is not going to be easy for them. They are well trained in yesterday's skills and the managers have little relevant experience of operating in a market economy. Cost accounting is dubious, and concepts like depreciation, profit and loss, source and distribution of funds and balance sheets, are alien to the majority of the people. In much of Eastern Europe the problems of ownership are still unclear, and the question of ongoing liabilities for environmental and other claims are still in the air. However, if you are really determined to make the attempt, you should continuously bear in mind that the future development of these countries is bound to be very uncertain. It takes a strong stomach, and a great deal of strategic faith, to launch oneself into this maelstrom – and yet out there somewhere there is great opportunity.

Many potential investors in Eastern Europe have found it easier to start up on a greenfield basis, rather than struggle with the legacies of the past, both in plant and attitudes. There is quite a lot to be said for this approach, but no one in their senses would try to go it alone. Strong partnerships are needed, for in a situation where everything is in a state of flux, it is the personal networks that hold these countries together. Indeed, at present, they are almost the only functioning systems. At this stage it will inevitably be very difficult for you to select the partners who really can, with your help, be the long-term victors in their home market. You must choose them carefully, partly because it is so hard to know what kind of qualities are actually going to be required, but also because, for the foreseeable future, these personal networks are going to continue to be vital. The key to success must lie in minimising the exposure to which you are committing yourself – whilst trying to manage the expectations of your partners. It is not reasonable for you to assume that your partners will view their own contribution in the same starkly realistic way that you will. Until as recently as two years ago most of them were fêted as the business leaders of their own countries, and in some cases of the Eastern Bloc. Moreover, for years they had all been told that the Eastern Bloc was superior, in almost every way, to the West. The harshness of the reality is difficult for them to grasp. It is going to be hard to keep them interested, unless they feel that there is a pot of gold waiting out there somewhere for them. At least this possibility will balance their disappointment at the low valuation which you are likely to place on their current offerings.

Building up trust and mutuality of respect is unbelievably difficult under these circumstances, particularly when words, even in translation, do not necessarily carry the same meaning. We have almost no shared values and very little understanding of each other's different worlds. Under these circumstances it is all too easy for each side to reach a misunderstanding – or even to apparently agree on mutually inconsistent premises. Accusations of dishonesty and impropriety abound, therefore, and even when cleared up they leave a lingering aura of suspicion and ill will. It is not much use working on the principle of *caveat emptor* under these circumstances. There is already plenty of *caveat* around, and the only solution is to underline the down side of any agreement to your partners in the hope that the inevitable nasty surprises can be minimised.

I do know a number of firms who have succeeded in developing businesses on this unpromising and stony ground. Most have either been in services, where the key is to find customers with the ability to pay, or in simple technology, involving the application of Western know-how and operating experience. Some successful relationships have been built on contract manufacture, where the products are sold largely outside the Eastern Bloc and the connection is really that of a selling, distribution and specifying organisation with a closely linked, but independent, manufacturer who is acting purely as a source of product. There are examples of where such relationships have worked to the benefit of both parties, because the selling arm has acted more and more as a spur and specifier to the production side. It is fatal to generalise for, even more than in most business situations, each country is totally different – with its own variety of strengths and weaknesses. Even within each country there is no such thing as a typical firm, and the personal variations in management attributes and skills are on a wider scale than we are accustomed to meeting. The incompetent are breathtakingly so, whilst quite modest successes, by our standards, are signs of Herculean endeavour, determination and courage.

Both in the EEC and in Eastern Europe it is depressingly easy to be sucked into a financial and managerial black hole. We come back to our old friend 'focus' and the necessity to concentrate effort on a very narrow front. This skill of concentration and determination does not sit easily with the ability to cut one's losses and run if the cause becomes hopeless, which is also absolutely vital. All this is made more difficult because of the new and attractive opportunities of which you become aware – usually just as the going becomes really hard. It is debatable whether medium and smaller sized companies should attempt to pursue opportunities in the single market and in Eastern Europe at the same time. My own view is that, unless you see Eastern Europe as a back-street way into the single market (for instance by developing in the former East Germany), the single market must take priority. It is tempting to deceive yourself into thinking that one of your people can pursue the longer term opportunity – with only occasional support from the boss. In reality, however, joint ventures and partnerships are made at the top and must be sustained by the top. It is essential to develop shared ownership of the concept at every level of contact, but the whole thing depends on the involvement of, and frequent tending by, the leaders of both enterprises.

One of the major considerations during the nineties will therefore be how the business leader allocates his own time and attention, and how he sets his priorities. In addition to being a tender flower, cross-national ventures are, by definition, time consuming. Relationships must be fostered informally, as well as on a business basis. This can often involve evening entertaining and nights away, and makes the idea of flying in and out in a day not such a good one. It is probably best to concentrate on getting experience of working with a country in the single market before venturing on to the wilder shores of Eastern Europe. The first is urgent, because that is where the competition is going to come from. The opportunities that are opening up in Eastern Europe will probably be far slower to develop than most people are assuming.

If you have decided on the EEC, and done the studies I referred to earlier, as well as 'walking the floor' and visiting the countries that appear logically most promising, you can now allow yourself the luxury of a little personal emotional bias. I firmly believe that doing business in a country is made much more difficult if you do not like the place and its people. Everything you do in Europe has to be done with a long-term view, and it is most unlikely that your preferences and prejudices will not obtrude at some stage. Moreover, business is about communication and trust, and neither of these is possible without emotional involvement. Inevitably you are also going to have to spend a lot of time in the country of your choice. There is not much future in that if you can't bear the food, and are continuously watching the clock in case you can get away on an earlier aeroplane. Many business people think that these things don't matter and that, in any event, you will grow closer to the place over time. This may be possible in some cases, but there is at least an evens chance that propinquity may fan dislike as easily as it may inspire love.

Now that you have selected the country of your choice (for which you have a warm glow) your next requirement is to find a national of that country who will run your business for you. It is adding another avoidable risk to try and operate in, say, Germany or France with a British manager, who will inevitably not be so familiar with the mores and business habits of the country in which he is to operate. There could hardly be more differences in the ways in which business is done than there are between Germany, Italy, Spain, Greece and Norway. We readily accept that we need a Japanese to do business in Japan, or a Chinese if we are to succeed in Taiwan, and yet we still think a smattering of a language will enable us to do business the British way in any European country you can name. If you think of this in its most basic fashion, even if you are familiar with the patterns of business, every contact for you is a new one and has to be worked on, whereas the German has a lifetime of contacts and friends which he can draw on.

The ways in which business is conducted, and especially the ways in which sales are made in the various countries of Europe, are not better or worse than our own habits, but they are certainly different, and if you are to succed that difference must be respected. When a Portuguese tells you that he can't meet you to discuss your deal until midnight, he means just that. He isn't trying to put you off – rather the reverse. If you want to do business you'd better be there – even if your plane leaves at seven a.m., and you wonder whether you'll get any sleep at all. German buying managers expect lavish levels of entertainment – of a kind which British buyers would view as attempts at bribery – but that's the way business is done in Germany. A cup of coffee and a hamburger at McDonalds will merely display to him your own lack of understanding and the poverty of your interest.

One of the biggest problems in all of this is pace and timing. If you are only embarking on this voyage you know that you are already late. You are therefore in a hurry and the tendency will be for you to try to make up for your tardiness by pushing harder and faster to catch up. This will be a mistake. These sorts of relationships cannot be hurried, and there is a real risk that attempting to push the process along will only lead to even more delays in the long run. Not everything can be made to work, no matter how much skill and patience is deployed, and the kind of pressure that a need for speed produces can cause all kinds of misunderstandings and mismatches of aspiration to appear. One of the most difficult problems is to know when and how to cut your losses and start again. In the heat of your courtship it is a sound principle to discuss the divorce procedure and settlement if things don't work out. The mere act of having done so increases the probability that it won't have to be used, but disentangling a joint venture which has gone sour is one of the most depressing, destructive and difficult tasks you can undertake in business. Emotion drenches the negotiations, and bitterness and disappointment are ever present. It is great news for lawyers but not much use to you or your shareholders. The other area to explore as frankly as possible at a very early stage in your relationship, is what the long-term aims of both parties are thought to be. It is inevitable that these will change over time, but if at the start there is notional acceptance of where you both hope to end up, the long-term chances of success are far better.

One of the consequences of stretching out into Europe, which few people seem to think through, is the effect that it will have on the way you operate in Britain itself. Mostly, since it is our initiative to expand, we think in terms of all the things that we have to offer to them. If that is our attitude we are likely to miss many of the potential advantages on offer. Our ability to operate on a European level depends greatly on our willingness to change our time-honoured ways of looking at things in the UK. Many of these changes will be in the detail of operations – things such as our invoicing procedures, information technology, networking or working hours. It is vital that we get away from the idea that we should be teaching those 'garlic eaters' the alleged superiority of British ways, and try instead to get everyone, throughout the business, to embrace the idea of becoming Europeans themselves.

British people tend either to dismiss the cultural and linguistic differences altogether, or build them up into such bogey-men that they resist the attempt to overcome them at all. This is curious, because when we go on holiday we are able to enjoy these differences and appreciate the many good aspects that other countries have to offer, whereas in our business contacts, partly through fear, we tend to distrust and misinterpret the same characteristics which we applaud when we visit a country on a private basis. The keys to resolving this conflict are time, sensitivity, patience and continuous reiteration by both parties of the desirability of the ultimate goal. There are some nationalities with which it is very easy to 'level', and to discuss worries directly and without prevarication – the Dutch spring to mind as being outstanding in this respect. There are others where a more gradual approach is necessary. The fact of the matter is that the prize is so vital that we must apply ourselves to the problem, but the key lies in realising that informal time spent with your European partners is a critical part of the whole process. I have never been one who believed that it is always a good thing to combine one's business and personal lives but, in the case of Europe, it is very frequently expected by the company with which you are dealing, and will certainly pay off immeasurably. The natural tendency of British business people has been to put to one side anything which takes up their time, but does not have a clear goal. Business relationships in Europe need to be looked upon as a marriage, and only a fool would hurry a courtship. In order to operate across national barriers and cultural differences, business requires even greater levels of trust than are necessary with a single country. As soon as misunderstandings begin to arise it is of the greatest importance to try to ascertain that you are both understanding each other clearly. Despite that fact that your grasp of each other's language is imperfect, it is depressingly simple to believe that each of you is attaching the same meanings to the same words, and that therefore you are in some way in the grip of a deliberate deceit. More often than not the problem derives from a lack of putting yourself in the other chap's shoes and trying to think your way through the position from his point of view.

Going wholeheartedly into Europe, therefore, adds to the

pressures on change and the persuasiveness of the vision. It can open vast quantities of new doors to your people. These days there are very few British people who have not visited the mainland of our continent, and yet working with people of a different nationality, on a day by day basis, is still an excitement in itself. In Britain we still instinctively think of Europe as being 'foreign', whilst America is seen as being less so. Few views could be more false – enhanced as they are by our illusion of a shared language. Both European and British companies encounter exactly the same difficulties operating in the USA as they do in each other's countries. In Britain this constantly surprises us, but in reality the culture, expectations, use of language, motivations and aspirations are as foreign in the USA as they are in Austria or Italy. British companies nevertheless look more readily to the US than they do to Europe, but during the nineties they will do so at their peril. Europe is where the action is and with the demise of communism, it is going to be where the growth is for many years. Companies who cannot think and operate as European ones will be few and far between by the beginning of the next century. It is not yet too late to start learning the skills, but it soon will be.

6 Those Bytes

The nineties are going to be the period of management paradox. So many things that we have believed but failed to act upon in the past are going to turn into things on which we shall need to have a change of perspective in the nineties. Nowhere is this more the case than in the use of information technology. The seventies and eighties were really the decades during which all of us believed that information technology would resolve all our problems. Our concerns were very largely linked to maintaining our place in the race. Were we investing in information technology fast enough? Were we investing a large enough amount of money compared with our competitors – as though the mere application of money in itself would somehow give us an advantage? It was in the 1980s that Professor Michael Scott-Morton pointed out that it was impossible to obtain a sustainable competitive advantage through the use of information technology. He pointed this out just at the time when most of us were investing heavily in ideas such as Electronic Point of Sale, in the belief that this action alone would place us a jump ahead of our competitors. From a depth of analytical research Michael pointed out that, although it might temporarily put you ahead of the game, all that it gave you was a head start. The mere possession of the technology was not enough. There seemed to be a feeling that a plateau of advantage could be gained by information technology. This erroneous belief appeared to spread because of the sheer amounts of money involved. More and more pressure was put upon hapless companies and managers to invest, with less and less consideration given to what would actually be gained and how such investments would change the way that the business was done.

I believe many of the problems of this period were caused because of the communication gap which existed in large, and even in some small companies. One only has to observe the way in which young people at school use information technology as an extension of their intelligence to see the vast gap that exists between those of us who have grown up with it and those, like myself, for whom information technology is a sort of updated slide rule. Of course the main feature of the slide rule was that you had to formulate a calculation in your mind in order to produce an answer. Almost the first management tool I was ever given was a slide rule and I quickly owned them in a battery of sizes, of varied transportability. In those days it seemed nearly impossible to deal with any management problem without a pocket slide rule, even though we were able to use mental arithmetic – a skill and facility which is often missing in the present generation. One of the key management skills has always been approximation. Tremendous accuracy is seldom required if one is using information to take decisions. What one is looking for is major differences rather than minor nuances, because time spent in adjusting to minor nuance is almost invariably time wasted. In itself, management is a pretty coarse activity and has to be applied on a substantial scale if it is to make any real impact. The major decision makers in companies were therefore brought up without familiarity with information technology and, although most of us did courses in our later years, our minds still find it extraordinarily difficult to realise the flexibilities and opportunities that advances in this field offer us in management terms. Curiously though, the concepts of continuous improvement and continous change which are now hallowed in Japanese tradition and are fast becoming the 'in' management theories of the nineties, were actually the basis of the management which I was first taught in the fifties. During the seventies and eighties, information technology was used almost exclusively to 'mechanise' operations which had hitherto been done manually, or by the application of people power. Surprisingly, and to everybody's concern, the expected explosion of productivity did not occur. It did not occur for two reasons. Firstly, people were slow to adapt to the new methods and secondly, these new methods tended to produce a barrage of information, which in turn took even more people to analyse and use it. Nothing is more useless or infuriating than asking a simple management question and getting the response delivered to your desk in the form of several hundred yards of computer print-out. Management is about concepts, and numbers are a vital part of establishing that one's concepts are in scale, relative to each other. Unless you have a very particular type of mind it is extraordinarily difficult to derive a concept from page upon page of densely packed figures which are accurate to three places of decimals.

The boards of most companies pursued a sort of dialogue of the deaf with their Information Technology Management during the seventies and eighties. Hopefully the top management knew what they wanted to achieve and the information technologists knew what the information technology was capable of. Neither side was able to appreciate the totality of the picture and this was not helped by the almost impenetrable jargon used by most I.T. trained people. The trouble is that they love their skill and are absorbed by the technological possibilities, as well as the ever increasing scale of what is possible. One only has to pass a simple management request to an I.T. man to see his eyes glaze over and watch him seem to disappear into a totally different world of bytes and megabytes. Frankly, most managers could not care less. Above everything, they do not want to be told that yet another new system will have to be bought. They also do not want to be told that, in any event, the system will be incompatible with everything that they already have and that the entire investment (which has been put in at enormous expense, and a marked effect on their profits) has been invalidated by this new and totally unreasonable request.

All of this makes it even more alarming that the imaginative use of information technology is going to be one of the key enabling mechanisms for business success in the nineties. Neither precedent nor our background abilities in the use of I.T. offers much encouragement that we are going to be in a position to come up with the feats of imagination and creativity which will be required of us. Those with the best chance are probably the younger people who have used computers to help them through their university studies and have now risen to a position where they understand the management challenges and tasks ahead. The problems of adjustment to the possibilities of this whole new world will reduce with the passage of time. By the next century it will be almost impossible to have someone at the head of a company who has not grown up with computers to assist them in a whole host of business and personal activities. The widespread use of electronic personal organisers, lap-top computers and word processors are all encouraging signs of a change from computer myopia to a new and brighter world. But in the meantime, the nineties will still find all too many of us, who are not 'computer comfortable', struggling to get our minds around the changes and possibilities that lie ahead. It does not increase one's confidence, however, when one realises that even the computer companies themselves are only using a small part of the technology that is available today. In the last five or six years I have asked practically every computer company how much of today's technology they are using in their own operations. I have yet to meet one who can claim to be actually applying more than sixty per cent of what is available.

The problem is made more alarming because, on present trends, the amount of computer technology which is available will double within the next three to four years. As I pointed out in an earlier chapter, it takes organisations about five years to adapt to new ways of working and if we start behind even before the technology increases, what chance have we of catching up? The answer, I fear, is very little unless we can build in to our management thinking and planning entirely new concepts of how information technology can change the business.

At this stage I should hasten to say that I am one of those aged souls who is not an information technology buff. My daughter has to resolve the simplest problems for me. Fortunately she is self-taught, and therefore does not immediately disappear in a cloud of impenetrable jargon. Between us we spend much time discussing what new gadgets or ideas can make our business life together easier and more effective and I am constantly surprised how well up with the forefront of technology we seem to remain despite our lack of formal training. Practically all the major trends that are occurring in business can only be followed and exploited if an information technology strategy is part of the total picture. Barely a point has been raised in this book so far which does not demand a different approach or use of one's computer systems, if one is to be in a winning position. The irony is that practically every board and chief executive that I know spends a good deal of time discussing the computerisation of their companies, and their prime concern seems to be whether they are spending as much money as the competition.

There are few, if any, comparative guidelines available to measure the effects of good use of computers. As a result you are almost always trying to catch up on the wrong area. This whole situation is going to become even more marked as open systems make it possible to introduce a form of continuous improvement into one's computer world. This will avoid the present situation, where you always seem to be trying to join a moving staircase, and doing so by a series of giant leaps. As soon as you arrived where you had aimed to be you find that it is the wrong place and you have to change everything around yet again. As well as being hideously expensive in people's time and money, this is a singularly inefficient way of managing a key competitive resource. While Michael Scott-Morton is right, and it is not possible to have sustainable competitive advantage through the application of computers, it has certainly been demonstrated over and over again that it is all too easy to have a self-accelerating competitive disadvantage. Once one gets substantially behind the competition it becomes almost impossible to try to catch up with competitors who are on faster and faster accelerating trends. Apart from being a recipe for going mad quickly, this also has major costs and operating disadvantages and you speedily fall into a sort of spiral of decline.

There is probably no such animal as a sustainable competitive advantage, but people who use computers to fundamentally change the way that business is done and the mindset of everybody in business, are likely to make a giant leap ahead of the competition which, if continuously reinforced, will enable them to stay ahead. Information technology in the nineties must be used not to mechanise, but rather to change the entire way in which business is done. There are myriad examples of where people have seen the possibilities that computerisation offers and have seized the initiative in entirely new areas of business, perhaps because there seem to be more opportunities in someone else's field than in their own. Even the most free-thinking of us tends automatically to accept constraints in the way that our own businesses are operated which, to somebody from outside, can appear incongruous and myopic. It is the really big 'why do we have to do it this way' question that can make the massive difference.

So many of the things that I have referred to are only possible through the use of computers. The whole approach of 'just in time' manufacturing depends critically on computers and computer links. The release of money thus engendered is far greater than the savings from computerising the payroll. People are only just beginning to realise that computer databases on clients' preferences and tastes offer them a competitive advantage if properly harnessed. Airlines have only recently realised that their computer systems offer them a major source of competitive advantage, not only in terms of revealing their customers' needs and requirements, but also in optimising fare structures and schedules. Indeed, American Airlines makes far more money from its computer systems than it does from operating its aeroplanes. It is at least arguable that the airline of the future will not operate aeroplanes at all, but will consist of a strategic planning, marketing and operating control system. Computer and information technology must be embedded right in the heart of your business. Increasingly the business should be designed around the opportunities that computers can offer, both organisationally and in terms of meeting customers' needs, rather than looking on them as part of the administrative machine.

One of the reasons why so little has been done in this area, apart from the impenetrable jargon, has been the tendency to allocate the responsibility for computers to the accountancy profession – as though their entire role was merely to be a part of cost accounting. It is important to make the use of computers a part of the whole business, rather than being a peripheral service to a business which is still organised conceptually and operationally as it was before these invaluable tools became available. The impact of information technology is at its most striking when the whole business approach changes to take account of the possibilities which it offers. It also offers the key enabling devices for changes in the costing system, business relationships and internal organisation, which are likely to be more in line with the personal needs which people have for growth and headroom.

One of the striking changes that began to occur in the late eighties was the recognition that verticality of itself is the most dangerous form of organisation you can have. For many years I served in a company that believed that verticality represented the ultimate optimisation of a business. The trouble is that the strength of any chain does not only depend on the links in the chain but, above everything else, on the links with the ultimate customer. When so much capital has been deployed all down the line it is very difficult for the person nearest the ultimate customer to remain in control of everything that stands behind him. Rigidities are inevitably built in and all the pressures generate the wrong way.

The horrors and pains of dismantling vertical companies, in order to introduce more flexibility and responsiveness into the system, have been well recorded. However, what is not so readily recognised is that forms of flexible alliances, which are the way we are trying to move for the future, depend critically on information technology for their effectiveness. A chain of companies can only succeed if it is faster than its competitors. To be faster than its competitors it needs almost instantaneous communication between each link. In each part of the chain it must also have the freedom to adjust to the information that it receives with maximum speed and effectiveness, without waiting for unseen heavenly hands to instruct it. In reality this means that everybody has to have access to information, which changes the relationships between companies in fundamental ways.

The old concepts of competition and competitive advantage were very largely based on the control of information. When I was trying to sell heavy chemicals I still remember my horror when I was faced with skilled buyers who had reconstructed my cost sheet with a fair degree of accuracy. Obviously this is still going on today, but the cost of playing this sort of buying and selling version of blind man's bluff is really not worthwhile, and it certainly does not enable either party to maximise the opportunities which are available to them. Today we see suppliers and customers working together much more, so that they can derive the maximum advantage from their combined business positions. This effort is hindered by secrecy, but it can be greatly helped by information technology linkages – very frequently on line.

The true advantage of Electronic Data Interchange does not lie in the saving of cost on invoices, even though no one in their right mind would turn down the reduction in countless pieces of paper. It does not even lie in direct debiting, desirable and helpful though this is to both parties. The real advantage of Electronic Data Interchange is that it enables supplier and customer to be in each other's minds, each looking after their own part of the business. With luck, and with a good relationship, they can help each other to achieve the ultimate advantage in the marketplace. This involves massive philosophical and attitudinal changes. The customer is no longer your enemy, but indeed your best hope. The relationship between you is no longer one of conflict but of collaboration. The end result is that both of you grow richer together because, if you persist in the bad old ways, you will inevitably grow poorer together.

None of this prevents the profit margins moving up and down the chain. There are still tremendous advantages in being 'the fastest with the mostest'. Those who maintain the highest rate of change will always have an advantage over their competitors, but the realisation that our ultimate profit rests both with good suppliers and good customers has been a slow one to come. It is, however, one of the most gratifying changes in business attitude that has occurred during my years in business. The technology to help us achieve these relationships is already there, and with open systems it will become even simpler. The problems to be overcome are very much more ones of ingrained attitudes to business and computers than they are of technical capacity. The habits of wishing to do a good deal within your established chain of supplier and customer, rather than looking at the competition, are hard to overcome and require changes of perception almost as large as those required to realise what the technology can make possible.

If you look within your own organisation you will almost certainly find even more striking examples of where technology can change everything, if only the mindset of the management will allow it. The proportion of labour costs involved in most manufacturing enterprises today is relatively small – in many cases under ten per cent. The opportunities to make major cost savings by moving to areas where the cost of labour is lower are in many cases far outweighed by the problems of training, back-up and flexibility which such areas offer. It is ironic how slow our costing systems have been to adapt to the changes that have occurred. In a world where the true costs of operating increasingly lie in what are euphemistically described as the 'overheads', we still measure production with extreme accuracy, while estimating overhead allocations almost on the basis of a finger held to the wind. The change to activity costing, which I believe to be one of the most fundamental changes offered in accountancy, is a management skill which invariably develops slowly. Activity costing attempts to allocate the areas of costs involved in research, marketing, technical service, customer service, product design and so on, considerably more accurately into the end costs. This is only made possible by the application of information technology, which in turn forces, or at least coaxes, people towards changes in organisation – and in a way the circle is completed yet again. The concept of small, self-contained groupings, where the costs are transparent, becomes a natural corroboration of the application of activity costing.

Professor Michael Porter pointed out that the companies and organisations which will obtain competitive advantage are those who can take an holistic view of their business, since progress and speed evolve from trading off perfection in one department in order to achieve a better result across the piece. This is a long cry from the days when large organisations grew by trying to divide the functions vertically, and to ensure that each function was as efficient as it could possibly be. Anyone who runs a small business knows that this denies the reality of business. In a small business one is constantly sacrificing the optimal best in one area in order to achieve whatever is required in another in order to make more profit. Large organisations, with their rigid departmental boundaries, internal politics and constant ability to take their eyes away from the ball which is in play, are all too prone to fall into this trap. Taking an all-round view of a business situation is not just a matter of willingness to sacrifice narrow departmental advantage for the greater good. It is not even a matter of having the confidence in one's own side that such actions will be recognised and rewarded. It is simply not possible to take a broad view of business unless information is easily and widely available. In large organisations the possession of information represented power, and secrecy was often justified against spurious grounds of commercial confidentiality. I am not so foolish as to believe that every organisation can work on the basis of total openness, but I am constantly amazed by how much information is held close to people's chests for reasons which have little or nothing to do with winning the competitive race. Here again information technology is the enabler, but human nature and previous beliefs and practice are the enemy. Many years ago I remember explaining to some of our continental competitors that I believed that the state of a company's business should be made available to all of its employees. They were appalled, being convinced that such openness would be instantly used to the company's disadvantage by its employees.

One really has to have a different attitude to openness if information technology is to perform the role that it so magnificently can. One has to trust and believe that others are as interested in the success of the business as you are yourself. After all, their futures and those of their children rest even more with the success of the whole business than they do with that of each individual department. It is not very easy to imagine the best cost accountancy department in the world existing in limbo. We are all interdependent, and much of our business success depends on our ability to work together faster and more effectively.

In the nineties the realities of these external pressures for total success are obvious to even the dumbest of individuals. There have been more than enough examples of people sinking to finally puncture the view that swimming on our own is easier than staying on board. These concepts lie very close to some of the contemporary thinking on organisation. Tom Peters' book *Thriving on Chaos*, and the efforts of many business leaders towards producing flat, non-hierarchical organisations, have all been assisted by the availability of information through imaginative and creative computer programes. Both the need for speed and the need for people to create their own personal business environment rather than reacting to instructions from above force moves towards delegation and decentralisation. Yet again computers can be either friend or foe. The problem is that the massive flow of information enables those who have a yearning to meddle to interfere and double guess almost every decision that can be taken. Computer programs are a continual invitation to top management to interfere. The ability to see, minute-to-minute and day-to-day, what every member of the tribe is doing, calls for tremendous acts of self-restraint on the part of those in superior positions. It also calls for a considerable belief in the ability of the troops themselves to do a better job than you can. It is human nature that this should be a difficult attitude for us to take, but it is the one which will differentiate the men from the boys in the nineties.

The trouble is that all-encompassing though information technology may be, it will always convey facts and numbers either instantaneously or after the event. What it does not convey is perceptions, beliefs and motivations. It is small surprise that we find it easier to hark back to the triumphs of yesterday and to believe that we can do the jobs of our subordinates better than they can – after all we were promoted for our excellence in their field. However, the world has changed since we were there, and the skills that we were able to use and the situations we dealt with are different today, and will be different again tomorrow. There is no way we can have enough information to take the decisions for the people who are actually involved in the battle. Sadly, very few business-men have been trained to have this degree of self-restraint, and the ability to see a continuously updated view of the battlefield makes it extraordinarily difficult to let people alone so that they can get on with the job in hand. These reasons alone are enough to encourage us to go for the sort of organisation in which every man and woman has a full-time job of their own to do, without having time available to spend 'supervising', 'coordinating' or just plain screwing up those who are actually fighting in the front line. The role of the bosses in the nineties is much more that of showing the overall direction and to coach but not to control. However, above everything else non-hierarchical organisations rely on the information which enables people to occasionally whirl above the battlefield and take a total view of what is going on, as well as doing their everyday jobs. Centralised organisations tend to pass all the messages back to the middle, which then deploys whatever resources or gives whatever solutions they think are appropriate. There are conditions under which this can be a good way to manage, but these tend to be ones where speed is not of the essence.

As I have pointed out already, the ability to change and react quickly is going to be essential in the nineties. This is going to be very difficult unless we are able continuously to see the totality of our operations. The problems of matching financial and business strategies, of trying to move quickly and to take risks, all require the ability to plug in instantly to the financial effects of different approaches and the understanding of what others are doing which will affect one's own activities and opportunities. The ability to survey the directions that your competitors and customers are taking, and the changes which they are making, are all key factors which enable decentralised operations to operate without any crippling loss of effectiveness.

How many organisations are actually thinking, working and organising in this way? I suggest all too few. I have believed for many years that organisations are upside down. In the past I have also written that it is the organisation that adjusts to the individual, thereby releasing the individual's energy, that will prosper. Nothing has changed in the nineties which should alter this basic view, but to operate in this way calls for readily presentable and assimilable information – not data. Computers make data easily available to everybody, but information is a different matter altogether. It is the aggregation and interpretation of data that enables decentralised organisations to work effectively. It is being able to tune into the dynamics of a changing situation that stimulates speed. All of these things are possible through properly designed and created information technology systems, but sadly too many of them are concerned with the transmission of raw data and too few with the interpretation of that data in ways which enable others to form their own deductions. The difference between data and information was strikingly forced upon my attention when serving in ICI. Initially, every quarter we used to receive a massive book, giving the detailed financial accounts of all our businesses, but these gave us very little feeling of the actual dynamics of the business. We found that each of us was spending long hours trying to interpret it, and realised that things would have to change. Imaginative pictorial computer programs projected the same data to all of us simultaneously, but it was presented in a wide variety of ways. Not only did these presentations save us tremendous amounts of work, but they also gave us a far better 'feel' of the events that were unfolding before us. This enabled us to contrast the actions of one business with those of another, and to understand the underlying causes and reasons why the cosy patterns of theory were not actually developing in practice.

During the Troubleshooter series I normally worked from the accounts of whichever organisation I was visiting. I was shaken when I visited one of the National Health Authorities to receive mountains of data but no information. Information works in almost inverse ratio to the quantity of paper that is transferred. This does not mean that in a decentralised organisation the individual does not need access to considerable amounts of raw data, which is the raw material of their business, but it is certainly not all that is needed. Since it is difficult to describe to others what they need to run their business, it is better to make sure that there is too much information rather than not enough. We need a sort of *smorgasbord* of information from which individuals can pick, but which is also backed by broad, dynamic and constantly changing pictures of the totality of the scene, analysed and simplified down so that the major trends are immediately discernible. Most organisations are investigating new and different approaches to organisation from those which they have inherited. The traditional hierarchical military approach will be even less applicable to the nineties than it was in the eighties.

Many of the future organisational trends have been derived from the vision and direction of businesses which have organised themselves around the possibilities offered by information technology. Professor Shoshana Zuboff of Harvard has outlined her concepts of concentric organisations, which already exist in the USA and is described in more detail in Chapter Ten. These ideas line up with an all too readily used word today, 'empowerment'. I believe strongly in empowerment, which is jargon for releasing an individual's ability and helping people to do their job as skilfully as possible. However, information support and understanding and clarity of goal are the absolutely essential mechanisms of empowerment. Hitherto our organisations have been all about control, and stopping people doing things – unfortunately information technology has been used as a mechanism of control for far too long.

In the nineties successful companies will use I.T. to help people to grow. Interesting experiments are being carried out to enable people to work from home. I do not work in an office, but from my home or hotel room, and a host of others do the same. They are using the new possibilities of information technology and improvements in telecommunications to work in their own time and in their own way, from wherever best suits them and their lifestyle. People who have been frightened of electronic home working because they believe that they need to control their subordinates more closely if they are to get the best out of them, miss the point. The great thing about electronic home working is that the only thing that is visible is the end result. Surely we should be paying people to achieve certain results, rather than to put in a certain number of hours? How they achieve these results and what time it takes them is largely up to them. My own experience of electronic home working is that in fact people drive themselves far harder than they are driven by their superiors. The knowledge that it is the results of your labours, rather than the efforts you put in, that are rewarded, is seen as a very powerful incentive to actual achievement. Electronic home working is going to make it possible for a host of diverse skills, which are at present under utilised, to be brought back into business possibly on a part time or occasional basis. Women with families can work from home. Retired people can be hired on a jobbing basis. Younger people will be spared the waste of time and hassle involved in commuting. All of these things become possible when those who do the basic organisation use a little imagination.

It is, however, a curious fact that when one telephones a man's office and is told he is working from home that day you tend to think that he is on a 'jolly'. It is perfectly possible to have the call instantly diverted, and yet how many people do this? The changes and advances that are occurring in information and communications technology are so far reaching that few of us have managed to get our minds around the freedoms they give us. Business success should be about exploiting freedoms rather than accepting constraints. The freedoms that are already available to us which we are not using are vast. If we could put only a small proportion of the effort we use in managing things in the same way as they have been for years, into thinking about how we could manage things tomorrow, we could make major changes which would help everybody. As always, the main problem lies with the top leadership of companies. People seldom take time out to think or discuss as a group how the business is actually done, rather than what is to be achieved. Since they take little time to think about what the organisation is capable of and how their people perform, it is hardly surprising that they spend so little time looking at the role that the information technology of tomorrow can play. Some of the major accents on how things are done relate to time that is spent and the back-up that people need. Increasingly, with the way that information technology and computer costs are developing, networking is seen as being a salvation, and indeed networking has transformed the costs of operating in imaginative ways. The difficulty is that networks, instead of increasing flexibility, can all too readily become straitjackets of their own. Information technology is all too often seen as a rigid constraint, instead of a flexible liberator. The people involved in I.T. need to think in a more flexible way. We need a more modular approach, so that the building blocks can be assembled in a thousand different ways. We need pictures of how modern, changing companies will work in the future. The thing that is most certain is that in the future they will work quite differently than in the past. But the limitations on these changes really do not lie in the fields of technology, they lie in the creativity and imagination of people. Both those who have to do the work and achieve the results, and those who have the responsibility and task of directing them.

7 All Lights to Green

It would be trite to pretend that environmental concerns were not around in the seventies. Indeed, from my earliest introduction into manufacturing in the 1950s, concern about the environmental impact of our activities was always very high on our agenda. In those days, however, the difference was that the environment was felt to be a localised matter. It had not yet become a matter of global political significance, and it was not only the population at large who were blissfully unaware of the long-term effects of the combustion engine and of burning fossil fuels. Plainly, operating in the chemical industry, I was acutely aware that the by-products and wastes which we produced could have environmental effects. From its very early days my company had set the aim of ensuring that our performance exceeded that of any known, or likely, governmental standard in the countries in which we operated. In the United Kingdom our operations were controlled by the factories inspectorate and, peculiarly to the chemical industry, the inspectors of the Alkali Act. I still believe that this act was one of the most effective and balanced pieces of environmental legislation. Because it insisted on utilising the 'best practicable means', the effect was continually to tighten environmental standards at a pace commensurate with the development of technology. It could be argued that the act was reactive rather than proactive and that it therefore did little to drive the development of new 'ever greener' technology, but that side of the chemical industry was catered for by economic and competitive demands. For many years, when asked to describe the activities of my factories at Wilton, I used to describe them as a piece of chemical 'pork butchery'. This was because our aim was to utilise every last bit of waste and upgrade it by adding value and turning it into something useful. Not only was burning or otherwise disposing of any final residue potentially polluting, but it was also wasteful. Inevitably the residues that were disposed of contained chemicals of various sorts and, quite apart from the fact that I was brought up to believe that waste was in some way sinful, there is no question that the chemical industry looked upon any trace of a chemical going into effluent as another potential bit of competitive advantage being wilfully ignored. The layout and development of the factory at Wilton bore living testimony to this belief, for each plant was in some way linked to, and supplied by, the others and any end product which had to be actually disposed of was extremely small.

Nevertheless, even in those less well informed times, we were deeply conscious of the fact that we had to be 'good neighbours'. I have always believed that industries and factories operate by a sort of unseen and unwritten licence, which is given by the community in which the factory is located. Factories which consistently offend the senses of the people in their locality, be it by noise, smell, intrusion through the amounts of traffic involved, or anything which disturbs the tenor and quality of life, run the risk of stirring up a hornet's nest of disapproval. Even more to the point, they will probably be unable to attract the best people in the area to work for them. After all, who wants to be viewed by their neighbours as contributing to the despoliation of their homes and society? In those days, however, it was noticeable that the concerns about lack of employment, together with the presence of wealth creating factories, overcame many of the concerns which people now feel passionately committed to expressing.

In trying to write about the differences in management in

the nineties it is not part of my aim to trace the history of the green movement, or the events that have led to the constant increase in concern and expectation of the steps that responsible companies should take to preserve our planet for posterity. Nevertheless, one of the biggest changes that managers must face in this present decade is the necessity for an organisation, not only to respond to green pressures but also to seize the business opportunities which these pressures represent. The sad fact is that most business people have looked upon the continual barrage of environmental concerns with which they are faced as being a threat to their business and find it very difficult to view it as a potential opportunity. Enormous amounts of time and effort have been devoted to trying to persuade these green pressures to 'go away'. There seems to be a feeling that somehow those who are arguing so vehemently against the ways that things are being done at the present time are doing so out of ignorance of the economic consequences of their actions, and that a bit of active propaganda will make the problem disappear. Most of the reactions of industry have, in my view, tended to increase these pressures rather than mitigate them. Managers have consistently failed to grasp the fact that sincerely held beliefs become a force in themselves. Scientists in particular find it hard to accept that emotional convictions are just as valid, and deserve just as much respect and concern, as scientific facts. The beliefs which are held may run counter to contemporary scientific wisdom, but the fact that they are held at all creates political and other pressures. Even though factual argument may in time affect emotionally held views, it is very seldom that acceptance of the facts themselves will actually remove the source of concern.

Most people are all too aware of the limitations of science. Indeed, when one works in a science-based industry one speedily becomes aware of the great areas of ignorance which exist, despite the depth of our knowledge and understanding in those areas in which we possess a scientific foothold. In few areas does this apply more strikingly than in matters relating to the environment. During the past thirty years I have seen the arguments sway this way and that with regard to the impact of almost every environmental influence. Even the end results of our activities are themselves extraordinarily difficult to measure and quantify with accuracy – be it global warming, holes in the ozone layer, or the impacts of releasing substances into the oceans. Because of these uncertainties and imprecisions the arguments continue to rage with ever-increasing fury. Many industrialists and managers have taken the position that no action should be taken until the damage they are accused of causing is proven, whilst many of the protectors of the environment take the diametrically opposite view – namely that it is the responsibility of the industrialist to prove that everything that is done can be proven to be safe, or, at the very least, unharmful. Anybody who has struggled with the problems of trying to demonstrate that a newly invented medicine or pharmaceutical, which promises to be a boon to sufferers of some particular disease, does not have harmful side effects to the human body, will know the enormous difficulties of proving such a negative. The wonders of nature and different combinations and interdependence of climate, flora and fauna, geology and man-made interventions which go to constitute our planet are of even greater complexity and diversity. The search for absolute proof either of consequential effect or of lack of such effect, seemed to me to become increasingly irrelevant. What was needed was some better balance between the proven advantages and potential disadvantages of whatever it was that we were doing, but this concept has proved extraordinarily difficult to present to politicians, public or media as anything except a wish to cop out and evade one's responsibilities.

The argument continues, but it is one that the manufacturer and manager appears to me to be losing – largely because they look upon the whole issue as a threat to their continued business success, or indeed to the continuance of their business at all. Yet there is abundant evidence that individuals do in fact make a clear trade-off in their own minds between the advantages that known polluting activities offer them, and the potential disadvantages about which they are so vociferously and continuously reminded. Be it the use of the motor car, willingness to use unleaded petrol, willingness to fit catalytic converters, or the willingness to pay more for electricity by paying for the clean-up costs of high-sulphur coal, people express their own acceptance of the trade-off between the desirable and the economically practicable by their willingness to pay. This demonstrable reluctance to pay reinforced the widely accepted view of many business people during the eighties, that there was 'no money' in green issues, and that they represented a threat rather than an opportunity. Many businesses took this a step further by seeking to use environmental legislation as a form of protectionism. The enforcement of different environmental standards and requirements in different countries created yet another invisible barrier to free trade, and was actively encouraged in some countries and businesses. Others saw the imposition of very harsh and demanding environmental legislation within their own countries as being an 'unfair' cost imposition and therefore actively sought to ensure that the high standards pertaining in their own countries applied to others, even though they had different environmental circumstances and different approaches to legislative control. Of course there were some honourable exceptions to these breathtaking generalisations. Long before the nineties some business people saw that, in addition to being socially responsible, there were actual business opportunities to be found in adhering to very high environmental standards. Indeed the Body Shop, set up by Anita and Gordon Roddick, was based on that supposition, and has been a tremendous and well-justified success.

However, for most people, the advance of 'greenery' was something to be resisted or pandered to, rather than embraced. The curious feature of this is that people employed in industry and business are a microcosm of society as a whole. There is no reason to believe that those who express concern about environmental damage to our planet and our lives are exclusively limited to people from academia or the media. Many people employed in industry feel just as passionately about the need for change as the most pronounced activists in the green parties that were set up across Europe. And yet companies, while tightening up their reactions to external pressures, still saw this as a matter of bowing to the inevitable. It is my belief that the successful businesses of the nineties will require a major change in their attitudes to this whole problem. In fact I believe that one of the keys to a successful business will be an inner conviction that the pursuit of better, more environmentally friendly methods of production will bring business rewards in their own right. There are already examples, such as the replacement products for CFCs, the methods of laser printing of micro-circuit boards, and many others, which show that research and development effort devoted to environmentally more benign products and processes can give businesses the opportunity of a major lead over their competitors, who are still merely trying to clean up the disposal of their waste products. The ingenious uses for products and wastes which have been developed are in themselves a source of potential profit. Even at its simplest the heat generated from incineration of waste can be of financial value in its own right.

The point that I am trying to labour, however, is that these changes in approach must stem from conviction and belief, and that there must be a change of investment policy. Hitherto the bulk of investment has been aimed at trying to ensure that the 'licence to operate' is maintained. Many years ago I remember being involved in some heated debates about whether we should spend money to 'scrub' the plumes of nitrous oxide which we were releasing into the atmosphere. The plume was of a dirty yellow type and, even to the layman, it was unmistakably something nasty. It was possible to remove the colouring, although the actual pollutant would still be being ejected into the atmosphere. I recall arguing vociferously that to merely conceal the evidence of our activities was a con, and that we should instead concentrate any available money on trying to evolve better ways of reducing, or recycling, the oxides, so that it became unnecessary to shoot them into the atmosphere. There are already a stream of new and useful products being produced as a result of this type of approach. The replacement of peat by composted softwood bark or coir fibre, which is a by-product of copra production, is just one example of how a determined attempt to find substitutes makes possible the solution of yet another waste disposal product somewhere else.

These approaches to environmentalism require a much deeper consciousness of the environmental hazards of one's own activities together with a degree of lateral thinking which, in many cases, takes one far outside one's own field of activity. Perhaps small companies face the biggest problems of all, for they are often short on resources and are sometimes unwitting contributors to overall pollution levels. Here, new thinking and approaches are required and the results will probably come from the activities of people other than those who are involved with the actual production of the pollutants. It seems to me very unlikely that any individual farmer will resolve the difficult problems of animal slurry. It seems far more likely that this will come about either through the activities of government research organisations, or business people in totally different areas, who see business opportunities in developing appropriate technology. A great deal of this technology will not necessarily be of very advanced types. There is no particular magic in generating methane gas from waste, but there is very considerable skill involved in collecting and utilising the methane that is produced as a natural consequence of the dumping of organic materials. I believe that governments, responding to increasing environmental concerns expressed by the great mass of ordinary people, will actively seek ways of encouraging collaborative developments of this sort. There are major opportunities for the diversion of research from weaponry and defence activities into these areas. Moreover, many universities have the ability to harness technical excellence across wide-ranging fields of knowledge and activity. Sadly, the success of universities in commercialising the results of their cross-technological expertise has so far been relatively poor, but the development of science parks attached to so many technically based universities offers opportunities for development along these lines.

There are well documented and expressed fears about the lack of business opportunities during what is foreseen as being the lower growth environment of the nineties. The fact is that there are, and will continue to be, a myriad of business opportunities, but these are likely to be found in different areas. The world has plainly not yet reached saturation point in its demand for motor cars, but it does seem clear that, with technological advances which have prolonged the life of existing vehicles, changes in demand for cars are more likely to derive from changes in design or environmental acceptability. Sensible business people will pay much more attention to environmental concerns and the work of environmental scientists than they have in the past, but they will be looking for opportunities rather than threats. The sooner that environmentally desirable products are seen as having an enhanced validity in their own right, the sooner we will begin to apply the whole battery of business skills to resolving the problems which we have unwittingly created in the past. Perhaps there are business people who have deliberately ignored the consequences of their own actions, but I think there are very few of them. People tend to forget that the major victims of the pollution of a factory are those who actually work in it, or live nearby. These people have a much greater vested interest in trying to ensure that their businesses are operated cleanly and safely. Nevertheless, these legitimate concerns may well be suppressed in times of very high unemployment and of course it is common knowledge that familiarity can sometimes breed contempt. It is most difficult to generate continual concern for safety in plants which operate year in, year out, without accident – and after all this kind of concern is, ultimately, the only safeguard we have. Pollution not only costs money but cleaning it up tends to cost even more, and is, in itself, a waste of money. The efforts which are put into cleaning up the operations of dirty factories would bring a much faster and more effective pay-off if they were directed towards preventing the pollution in the first place.

Perhaps amongst the greatest culprits in this area has been the availability of large quantities of ridiculously cheap water. This has meant that we have all failed to value water as a worthwhile resource in its own right. We have tended to dispose of substantial quantities of undesirable waste products through the simple medium of dilution, rather than tackling the issues in a different way. It also seems increasingly likely that some form of carbon tax will be applied by governments seeking to respond to the clamour for action to reduce environmental pollution, as well as seeking new sources of revenue.

A deeply held conviction that it is necessary to operate in an environmentally better way can lead to a great many unexpected benefits, even though operating in this way is generally seen as being a distraction from the basic business of making money. For a start, an environmental audit of your activities involves looking at everything that you do in new ways. In theory the good businessman does this continuously, but in practice improvements are always incremental – and very seldom fundamental. Somebody who believes that they should 'clean up their act' will start by looking at everything that goes into the factory or office, and everything that comes out. Anything left over between the two is bound to be wasteful, and will also have to be disposed of in some way. We are increasingly beginning to realise that we cannot continue disposing of products – even if they are relatively benign – into land-fill sites. Anything that is not utilised constitutes a potential loss of profit, as well as actually costing money to dispose of. Companies which have begun to look at things in this way have surprised themselves by the substantial increases in efficiency which they have been able to achieve. Of course efficiency converts very quickly into money. It really is true that environmentally sound activities are, generally speaking, financially rewarding ones – although here, as in any other business action, the law of diminishing returns has to apply. Looking at one's business in this way, as well as being a worthwhile exercise in its own right, speedily leads on to a very different sort of approach to business.

One of the problems with pollution is the variability of the waste that is produced. In some instances this variability is caused by the natural variability of the raw material with which the operation starts. However, at the present time enormous efforts are being made to reduce this variability – even in natural products. The most obvious way of removing it is by careful selection and grading. Advances in technology are increasingly making it possible to produce replicable standards – even in items such as vegetables, cotton, and wool. These efforts pay off because of the reduction in levels of waste and the ease of processing consistent products. Well-run factories are those in which control is exercised at every stage of the changing of products or the working up of the process. The advent of microprocessors, together with the development of better sensing systems, gives opportunities of control which are totally different to anything which was available even thirty years ago. In turn these forms of control lead to greater consistency and quality of product.

It may seem a big leap from environmentalism to the well-publicised theme of quality but personally I believe that the two are closely linked. Quality management tends to have a threatening tone to it and, even though a great many companies are seeking quality management systems, in many cases they do so out of economic necessity, rather than inner conviction. Like many other developments in business, the concepts of total quality management have been developed in Japan – although they originated very many years ago, through the work of Deeming. Deeming, an American, is generally credited with being the father of concepts of total quality management. It was he who pointed out the indivisible connection between the ultimate quality of the product and the way in which the organisation was controlled and managed. It is this which is essentially the basis of all quality management systems. Increasingly the quality of end products is going to become not just a source of competitive advantage but an actual condition of operating at all. Large numbers of companies and organisations demand adherence to systems such as BS5750, as well as other quality standards. Increasingly it will be impossible to become a supplier of intermediates to others in the industrial chain unless you can show clear adherence to what have been hitherto regarded as impossibly high quality standards.

There has never been too much difficulty in the United Kingdom about quality. In many cases our best has been as good as, or even better than, the best in the world. In the UK the difficulty has always been that lack of control, and poor attention to detail, has meant that the consistency of our products has been extremely variable. Many years ago, when ICI started to supply chemicals to Japan, I remember that I could only do so by selecting the best from our run of production. Just as the Japanese approach to design, as exemplified in the development of the Lexus car, involves the sort of well organised and managed industrial processes which seek to achieve the raising of consistency and heightening of quality by ever-increasing degrees of control at all stages of the process, the basis of most quality systems has been to apply the concept of quality at every level of a company's operation. It usually starts by looking at the processes involved at the top, and then works the whole way down to the operations on the shop floor. As with an environmental audit, much of the value of the process comes from actually carrying out the operation itself. My local laundry was one of the first to apply for BS5750 and I was fascinated to see the tremendous difference it made to the attitudes of all the managers, supervisors, van drivers, and ladies who were involved in the firm. The common struggle of trying to achieve recognition in this way bound them together in a most effective way, and the sense of team spirit that emanated as a result was almost tangible.

In the future consistency of very high quality will be seen as the norm, and will virtually be taken for granted. Already the Japanese are looking for reject ratios of less than 0.1 per cent. Quite apart from the effect on the end product, the constant pursuit of quality also means a reduction of waste and of double working, all of which increase the use of capital and the efficiency of the operation as a whole. Even though I do not believe that quality as such will, in future, be a source of sustainable competitive advantage, there is no doubt that a reputation for quality, just as in all other forms of branding, is a priceless asset and one for which people will pay. The attraction of many luxury brands and goods lies not just in the 'snob value' of buying the best but also in the conviction that you are buying a consistency of quality and service which is not available in the mass-produced item. With the application of modern technology almost the reverse is true. In a modern, carefully thought out and managed production system the factory-produced object will always beat the hand-crafted item for consistency, and often for excellence. Anybody who doubts the changes in quality standards that are occurring need only look at the reliability of the modern motor car, the running life of the modern car tyre, the absence of necessity for watch repairs, the forgotten art of darning holes in socks, or the fact that, unless one's girth varies – as mine tends to do – the life of a modern shirt will often be ten or fifteen years. Many of these changes are not remarked upon because they are the result of continuous slow improvement and adaptation. Looking at one's business from an environmental point of view and following one of the total quality management systems causes one to ask fundamental questions about all the processes through which your products pass. In any event such an exercise is absolutely necessary from time to time, because it is very hard continuously to look critically at all aspects of your activities against the background of the technical and other developments that are occurring.

Another aspect of quality management in the factory has been the realisation that when operations follow on smoothly from each other there is a much better chance of consistency. I know of pottery manufacturers who are actively seeking to develop systems by which pottery is produced on a continuous assembly line, without interruption. Such systems do not just increase throughput, and therefore reduce cost, but they also reduce variability of reject rates and reworking. Once quality developments in one's own factory are approaching the point of diminishing returns, there are still improvements which can be made by looking at what happens to the raw materials, and also the stages through which one's products go once they reach the customer. Just as in your factory the consistency in quality is only as good as the weakest link in the chain, so in the chain of supply everything is interdependent and linked. The efforts which are made to achieve quality in the end product need to be reflected the whole way through the chain.

This concept of the interdependence of the chain of supply leads to fundamental changes in the relationships between companies, which I expand upon in a later chapter. Just as the pursuit of consistently high quality in one's own product depends upon eliminating variabilities and improving the quality of the starting ingredients (as any good cook will know), so the ultimate success of the entire endeavour depends, in turn, upon the quality, reliability and consistency of the distribution, wholesaling or retailing services. If I were to award a blue riband to the two companies which have improved most in quality terms in the past few years they would both be British. The quality of service on British Airways has been totally transformed over the past ten years, through enormous attention to detail, relentless training and continuous reiteration of the values of the organisation. The Rover Group have transformed themselves, not only in the way in which the business is run but in the quality and design of their product. They have done this by the involvement of everyone, and the ruthless overhaul of every system and concept which existed in the company. Although they gained from their association with the Japanese, and studied the Japanese approaches thoroughly, they did a great deal more than merely transferring Japanese systems into a British environment.

The companies who will succeed in the future are those which see their role as being to enhance the value of each stage of this chain. Equally well, much of the impact of producing environmentally friendly, high-quality and consistent products is lost if these are processed by people who are careless of such values and approaches. The train of thought and change of approach started by looking at one's processes through the eyes of the environmentally caring stretches a very long way indeed. In the nineties, when competition is going to be tougher and there will be more fundamental restructuring of industries than we have seen before, it is those who take these broader views, and seize the opportunities for beneficial change that they open up, who will survive – whilst others will inevitably, and expensively, go to the wall.

8 The Time Capsule

One of the realisations that has dawned on business people rather slowly during the last decades is the truth of the old maxim that time is money. I believe that there are a number of reasons why they had lost their grip on that eternal verity. Managing in a high inflation environment actually conceals the effects of increases in cost. Provided (and it is a fairly big proviso) you can survive in high inflation circumstances, no matter how expensive the plant you build it can always be shown to be the cheapest in pounds of the year. Inflation conceals a number of mistakes, particularly strategic ones. All of us who have operated in high inflation environments have learnt the lesson that one should not hold money, and that any available money should be turned into goods as quickly as possible – even though the goods might not be, strictly speaking, the most economical buy. As far as the processes of business were concerned, the penalties of mistakes and slow decision taking were often concealed, and the inflationary process tended to favour the large companies who, by definition, are more ponderous and slow moving than smaller, more highly delegated, organisations. A slowing of world inflation led to the realisation that enormous amounts of capital were tied up in every aspect of an organisation's work. The most obvious example of this abrupt realisation of the financial penalties of carelessness about time was the development by the Japanese of the 'just in time' system. In old-fashioned factories each machine or assembly point was characterised by a pile of raw material at one end and an equally impressive pile of finished product at the other. From time to time another load of raw material would be delivered and a quantity of the finished product would be moved on to its next destination. All this added up to an enormous amount of work in progress – and thus money tied up. Even assembly lines were supported by sub-lines of piles of materials which were waiting to be added to the product moving down the line. In theory, 'just in time' should eliminate all of this. By the use of information technology, each stage of manufacture is integrated into the whole – so, for instance, the wheel is produced 'just in time' to be assembled on to the car, which then moves on to its next stage. The theory has proved to be easier to describe than to actually achieve, but the potential savings which can be achieved by the careful organisation and control of production technology are immense. Not only is this system very much more efficient and flexible, but it can also release enormous amounts of capital which have hitherto been tied up at almost every level of long and cumbersome chains. Indeed, one of the paradoxes of life is that the Japanese, who first invented the system, are increasingly having to build up stocks in the pipeline because of the length and variability of delivery times – even from their quickly responsive suppliers.

The effects of the recession and the reduction in demand, combined with higher costs of real money than we have had to cope with for many years, place enormous penalties on the carrying of excess stocks, and there are equally enormous competitive advantages for those who operate 'lean and mean', in every sense of the words. It is the organisation that has low overheads and is quickly responsive – that makes to order, and can react quickly to customer demand – which has the best chance of survival in a recession. These approaches are being forced upon us by economic necessity – but they are a long way behind strongly held belief, throughout a company, that time does indeed cost money and that speed in an organisation is a source of major competitive and economic advantage. One of the difficulties is that for most of the post-war period we have been taught continuously to optimise, in financial terms, every step of the process, and to reduce every measurable expenditure. It has been this understandable belief in the logic of optimisation that has constantly led us to try to extend the chain of manufacture, so that we can control every step. The sixties and seventies were the heyday of verticalisation and the belief that it would be possible to operate every stage of the manufacturing process, through centralised control, in an optimal way. It was relatively easy to measure the theoretical savings to be made by controlling every step of the process. Indeed I remember that the pursuit of vertical integration in ICI inexorably led us back into oil and forwards into the manufacture of textiles, so that at one stage we controlled every step of the manufacture of a polyester shirt, apart from the growing and preparation of the cotton with which our synthetic fibres were blended. It was my immediate predecessor as Chairman, Maurice Hodgson, with his rigorous intellectual approach, who pointed out to me the consequences of this pursuit of optimum profit. Albeit unwittingly, we had created for ourselves the highest possible risk profile. We had piled more and more capital behind our hapless polyester shirts in a bid continuously to capture the added value at each intermediate stage from our original discovery of the oil. This was fine until the inevitable happened. The pressure of the amount of capital that we controlled behind the end product which went into the market-place, inevitably began to be felt right down the system, which became less responsive and increasingly dedicated to trying to sell what we could make, rather than having the whole chain responding to trying to make what we could sell. Certainly I have been seared by the experience of verticalisation and I believe that the current experiences of other companies who have followed this approach should be a salutary warning to every one of us. But it was not just the risk profile of what we had erected, it was also the fact that owning every stage of the operation lost us flexibility and time.

At that stage we did not actually value time – we were only concerned about it if we saw ourselves as being in a direct and identifiable race with a competitor who was trying to bring a product to the market. If there was no specific competitor, we were content to believe that, as long as we moved reasonably fast, nobody else would catch us up. The idea that getting to the market faster would, in itself, give us competitive advantage did not occur to us, and the concept of spending some additional money in order to give us a greater speed of reaction and more flexibility would have been alien to all our thinking. Indeed, many of the consequences of placing a value on lead time are ones which initially appear to be counter intuitive and potentially wasteful. At first sight the concepts of parallel manufacturing stages seem to be potentially less efficient than sequential manufacturing, and the concepts of parallel research and parallel development quite plainly add significantly to the cost. It is only if you believe that bringing your product to the market first will give you a greater lead time than the competition that you can possibly justify such apparently profligate approaches. And yet it is through these apparent inefficiencies that the time to market of new products has been slashed in practically every organisation. This is most clearly understood by the Japanese, who have for many years been concentrating on reducing the time to market of new products. You only have to look at the continuous string of 'new' products in the electronics field to realise how much the development times have been reduced. Those who see the saving of time as both a means of operating more effectively and potentially saving money will also be aware of the enormous amounts of time which are wasted in organisations through sloppy, slow and multi-staged decision processes. For example, in many companies an idea which originated in a factory will already have gone through the factory manager 'sieve' before going to the production manager, the divisional board – and even, in some cases, the main board. In the meantime it will have been discussed and criticised by the staff departments and will probably have been vetted by the safety department, the sales department and so on. Leaving aside the fact that such processes are inevitably a major deterrent to most managers – only the most determined of whom will be prepared to battle through layers of management, each with the power to say no – there is a real and measurable cost to such slowness of reaction.

Consultants who have studied these matters claim that significant savings can be made purely by the process of speeding up the decision time. There are many consultants who now specialise in looking at organisations, not from a theoretical point of view, but against the parameters of tracing the time involved – much as, in the days of method study, we charted the individual stages through which every decision process went. Of course there we were looking for superfluous and repetitious stages which we could eliminate, but measuring the time involved has much the same effect. As in practically everything else in business, this attitude to time starts at the top. The sense of urgency, time-scale of reaction and the standards set within a company for movement, speed and response are all a reflection, partly of the competitive environment in which you operate, but also of the values and standards which can only be set by the chief executive and board of the company. Even the most cursory examination of companies that have gone to the wall will reveal a common factor. All too many of them have been slow to respond, slow to change, and had got stuck in their ways. Probably the saddest example of this is the case of General Motors, who exemplify the exact opposite of a time based organisation. The present revoutionary changes which are being forced upon them by a combination of an extremely long decision tree and a slowness to respond to Japanese competition, developed from an in-born belief in their own superiority. In itself, speed of response not only facilitates the processes of change about which I have written earlier, but also arouses the kind of expectations and standards in the minds of the people in the company which are increasingly essential to success. Those who believe that time and speed are sources of competitive advantage will seek to organise decentralised methods, using small teams that can move fast, with a minimum number of layers between the top direction of the company and those who are responsible for the actual carrying out of the business. Speed and flexibility are actually synonymous. The advantages of trying to organise for speed are not only that you may get there quicker than the competition, with the attendant advantages, but that you can speedily recover from a taking a wrong direction.

However, this belief in time as a source of competitive advantage still remains just that – a belief. If they are not a part of the values of the entire company, it is very unlikely that any organisation will deliberately set out to achieve these ways of working. Indeed, many people seem to feel that speed is synonymous with carelessness and inadequate attention to detail. Moreover, the availability of modern information technology can, as I pointed out in Chapter Six, all too easily become a source of further reasons for intervening in decision making at all sorts of levels, and thereby losing speed. The irony is that, although information technology has given us the ability to decentralise and operate more speedily, unless efforts are made to utilise it in that way it can also be one of the most potent forces for centralisation, rigidity and control in an organisation. The risks of not moving fast far exceed those of actually doing so. As I have pointed out, the fast moving organisation can swiftly recover from mistakes or taking a wrong direction, whilst the slower and more rigid one still doggedly pursues its course. Moreover, the fast moving organisation can reinforce success very quickly, whilst the slower one probably has to wait until there has been a total reassessment from its command centre.

It is my belief that in the nineties enlightened managers and business leaders will look anew at every way in which their business is conducted, bearing in mind the value of time in a competitive sense. As an example of the kind of area where thinking has been affected by this belief let us look at the consequences of 'just in time' production. The concept of 'just in time' production involves very much closer and more flexible working between the supplier and the purchaser. Whereas General Motors and Ford in the States initially started as companies which sought total vertical integration, Japanese car manufacturers are specifiers and assemblers, rather than manufacturers. There is little difficulty in seeing which of the two philosophies appears to be winning at the present time. In theory at least it should be possible to operate a totally vertically integrated organisation in a 'just in time' mode, but in practice this is almost always extraordinarily difficult to achieve. This is partly because of the impossibility of re-creating the immediacy and pressures of the market-place within an organisation – even if transfer prices are conducted at 'commercial rates', but it is also because of the inevitable temptation for top managers to mitigate losses in one department by operating another in ways which are less appropriate to the end demand. The 'just in time' philosophy involves very close working between suppliers and customers at every level, but it leaves them to resolve the myriad of daily decisions rather than pushing such decisions up the line to others who will not feel the immediacy of the effect. The real gains to be had from 'just in time', as well as the freedom from interference, are the enormous amounts of capital which can be taken out of the chain at every level. Few companies charge their constituent parts for the use of working capital, which adds to the dangers that exist for the vertically integrated ones. No penalties are exacted for carrying excess stocks, which are often held in order to insure against the danger of running out, or to avoid the hassle of chasing up slow deliveries. In the days of inflation, companies often found that their excess stocks actually appeared to earn them money. Small surprise, therefore, that so many monolithic organisations found themselves stacked to the gunwales with, all too often, unusuable or dead stocks of intermediate goods. In independent chains of self-standing businesses which work together in the 'just in time' system, each one is looking at the totality of their own business situation and seeking to ensure that they are achieving their sales from the minimum amount of work in hand and minimum amount of raw materials held. 'Just in time' philosophy leads to closer integration of ordering and computer systems, and also to administrative savings, as well as the release of capital, and it is only a short step from there to move into joint development. This involves the supplier and the customer working together in a completely open manner on the development of a new product. The supplier will be working on the required changes in the items which he specialises in supplying at exactly the same time as the customer is developing the product of which they will be a part. 'Just in time' tends to produce degrees of trust and openness between suppliers, competitors and customers that enable the development of closer relationships in other areas.

It was the Japanese who first pioneered the idea of parallel development. At first sight it would appear to be one of the least effective ways of developing a product. To start two teams, with exactly the same developmental objectives, at almost exactly the same time should be a straight duplication of costs – and yet the competition and feeling that they are in a race seems to add to the sense of urgency felt by the two teams. This brings advantages which more than outweigh the additional costs, both in terms of the quality of the end product and the speed of delivery. Over the past ten years the time taken to bring a new product to the market has been reduced in most companies by a factor of between two and four, and in some cases as much as ten, by using these and other techniques. It is the people who can most speedily bring a product from the stage of conceptualisation to actually having it feeding the markets of the world who will ultimately set the pace which everybody else has to match.

There is an interesting clash of philosophies going on at the present time between German car makers and those of Japan. Typically the German car makers still take between two and three times as long to bring their product to market as the Japanese. In the eyes of the Germans this is justified by the thoroughness of their approach, and insistence on multiple testing before bringing products to market. The Japanese start the other way round, so to speak. They take the view that they have to bring the product to market more quickly, but feel that they have to have done all their testing, and have ensured that the product is flawless in performance, by the time it gets there. They achieve this by processes of parallel development, and the application of very large numbers of engineers, organised in small, self-standing teams. They gain speed by having the teams continuously working together in a collective way, which ensures that each one of them is able to cover for the other and is involved in all the stages of decision making – despite enormous pressure for speedy results. Many years ago my division of ICI built a chemical plant in competition with the Japanese. We were both building identical plants and decided to proceed at exactly the same time. Moreover, the Japanese had some of our people helping them. In the event the Japanese came into production, with a plant that worked, significantly more quickly than we did. When I looked at the reasons why, there appeared to be three. To my mind the most important was that the Japanese plant was built by a team which shared a single large office and lived, worked and dreamt together, twelve hours or more a day, during the whole time of the development and planning of the plant. They were each in each other's minds and did not have to send a memo, or make a telephone call, to check the effects of, for example, locating a valve somewhere else. Any one of them could cover for anybody else. Moreover, the whole lot were imbued with a sense of urgency and a determination to ensure that not only did their plant start up first, but that it worked perfectly. At that time there was not much difference in the numbers of people that we both deployed, but there was an enormous difference in the philosophy. We had started breaking ground much sooner than they had, and took solace out of commencing construction months before they began such activities. In their case no work started on the site at all until the total design had been carried out and the materials had all been provided on site. The result of this was that nothing had to be redone, and the construction period itself went like greased lightning. The second reason was that exactly the same team which had done the designing were also involved in the construction. There was no handover, no communication problems – the thing just flowed. These differences of approach stem from the belief in the value of time, and consistent efforts to ensure that time can be gained by reducing meetings, memoranda and reports to supervision. The third apparent reason why the Japanese plant got away so much faster than our own was that they had had the forethought to put a Shinto shrine in front of the plant. However, when I had one put in front of ours it did not seem to make up for the lapses in management that had led us to be so much slower and less effective in our own field of technology.

Those who value speed also believe in parallel development at both the research and the development stages. I know of cases where this has been taken a step further and the research department of one company works directly into the development teams of the people who will ultimately be suppliers. Modern technology makes the communication problem simple, provided the elements and atmosphere of trust and understanding are in place, and there is agreement on shared goals.

The appreciation of the importance of time and flexibility, coupled with the realisations of the interdependence of the chains, leads to totally different ways of relating to customers and suppliers. Like most things in business this is not something new, but the altered conditions of the 1990s, where competition and change are both more intense, can only be met by seeking to increase the profitability of the whole chain. In the days when I was a buyer, the relationships between the supplier and his customer were generally speaking adversarial, even though my own training was that there always had to be something left on the plate for the other man. Indeed I was taught that the greatest sin a buyer could commit was to run one of his suppliers into the ground and force his bankruptcy. However, in those days we thought primarily of continuity of supply and interruptions in that continuity – it did not occur to us to try to ensure that the whole of the supply chain was more effective and efficient than its competitors. It is only through maximising the profit of the chain as a whole that enough can be made to give each of the constituent parts of it a decent living. These efforts to gain competitive advantage for the whole chain are ones which call for changes of attitude, openness and trust between the constituent parts. Early on in my career I was lucky enough to be an indirect supplier to Marks & Spencer and I learnt a great deal from the experience. The policies which they pioneered, of trying to ensure that their suppliers were helped to be efficient and of the highest quality against the rest of the world, whilst ensuring that they still remained as suppliers, are now more generally recognised across the world. This appreciation of interdependence needs to be understood at every level. Building up the confidence of an organisation can sometimes lead to feelings of arrogance and superiority towards those on whom you are actually dependent for making a living, which can then lead to a lack of respect for the customer, or even the supplier. The 1990s is seeing the return of the importance of good relationships in business, despite the heightened pressures upon each of us to earn our livings in increasingly difficult circumstances.

There is another aspect of organisation and internal working in companies which is critically affected by the appreciation of the importance of flexibility and time. Michael Porter was amongst the first to point out that the more profitable companies were those that were able to take a holistic view of their business. Many of the trade-offs which are necessary to ensure continuous profitability have to be made between the different departments and functions in an organisation. Those who obtained their early initiation in business, as I did, in the 1950s were brought up in a world which believed strongly in optimisation of individual parts of large businesses. The company was therefore broken into vertical strands of organisation, each of which sought to be supremely efficient in its own right. Thus the production side was continuously monitored against production cost and urged to improve its unit cost, whilst the sales side was monitored against turnover. If you happened to be in one of the service sides of the company, such as purchasing and supply, accountancy or distribution, you were not only measured against your own previous best performance but, more specifically, against others in your own particular field. The belief was that if each constituent part of the whole was operated at its maximum efficiency the company's profit would automatically be high. Alas, like so many other theories, this proved not to be the case. The theory that high profits automatically appeared at the bottom of the chain was amply disproved.

Anybody who was lucky enough to have operated as both a manufacturer and a salesman at different stages of their career was all too aware of how large organisations contrived continuously to lob the ball of profit backwards and forwards between one and the other. In vertically organised companies of this sort it is odd how often it seems to happen that when the salesmen can sell more the production outfit cannot make it, or when the production outfit can make it the salesmen cannot sell it. The truth of the matter is that profit can only be achieved by continuously adapting, so that the achievement of profit is the ultimate goal and binding force between every part of an organisation. An adjustment of production schedules may enable the additional sales (and hence profit) to be made, even though you are apparently sub-optimising production. Selling something else, even at a lower turnover, but which the production people can actually make at the time is certainly better than the mindless pursuit of volume in its own right. However, operating in this way calls for different forms of organisation and value in the system, which are very difficult to obtain in companies which have always been run in old-fashioned ways. What is going to be needed for the future are specialists who are able to contribute their expertise in order to ensure that all possible opportunities for profit for the company as a whole are seized. Just as the search for optimisation of a vertically integrated company almost inevitably leads to trouble, so a company which seeks to optimise each individual function and activity will almost invariably be sub-optimised as a whole, and yet again the reasons link to flexibility and time. Obviously if you measure and reward people in particular ways they will almost always seek to play their own personal game at the expense of the team game. If you have been brought up to believe in excellence and perfection in your chosen field of specialisation it is extraordinarily difficult to aim for something which is less than the best, even if so doing will enable somebody else to reap the benefit. Endless attempts have been made to enable organisations to achieve these aims.

The most obvious examples of sub-optimisation have always been in the continuing battle between the geographic element and the product. Although most companies started in the clear position where those in charge of the product were responsible for marketing it throughout the world, the see-saw inevitably dipped and power moved to those in charge of smaller geographical areas, who could dictate what they wanted. The see-saw has, in most cases, swung back again and we are now looking at concepts of 'global management' of a particular product. In some companies this has been further complicated by a considerable negative power of decision on the part of the technical people as well. In the 1970s there was a vogue for matrix management, in which both the national company and those in charge of the product were conjointly responsible for the pricing and other decisions involved in making and selling successfully. The trouble with matrix organisations tends to be that nobody actually owns the profit and managers can satisfy themselves by keeping happy a number of different masters, each with different objectives and aims. It may genuinely be that, if you are to make the greatest profit in the long term, it is better to hold back your activities in one country or business in order to enable another, which has greater long-term potential, to move ahead. But, given the values which usually apply in most large organisations, these decisions are almost impossible to take, unless the company values the whole rather than the constituent parts.

This inability to look at their business in an holistic way is one of the reasons why small companies are usually able to run rings around the large. The small owner-proprietor has no option but to look at the whole of his business. It is very easy for him to hold things back on one side in order to encourage the other to achieve what he wants – which is more profit. When I took over as Chairman of ICI I was astounded to realise that I was the only person in the company who had the ultimate organisational responsibility for the profit of the entire company. Of course to a degree this responsibility also lay with the board of directors, but we were organised in such a way that each member of the board was responsible for looking to their own individual bits of the company and trying to optimise their activities – rather than seeking to manage the trade-offs that were necessary if the company as a whole was to prosper. In a smaller way this same problem appears at every level of large and complex organisations. It is partly because of the difficulty of getting organisations to operate in an holistic way that people have been moving away from the concept of doing everything for themselves. It is not only market forces and the spur of competition that makes it increasingly unwise to run one's own 'in house' catering, for example. Leaving aside the problems inherent in developing expertise in this sort of area, it is also difficult to provide adequate career opportunities for those who rise to the top of this kind of specialised field in a company whose primary business is not in the catering field.

Managing in an holistic way means that we need a number of organisation enablers, as well as changes in values. We need more and more 'helicopter pilots' who, from a basis of technical competence in their own field, can scan the whole business horizon and understand the contribution made by others. We all recognise the problems of companies where the specialist functions have developed so much expertise in their own field that they create a kind of life of their own. Many companies have sought to resolve this problem by hiving them off as separate businesses, or alternatively getting out of the business altogether and, for example, getting their computing done by a specialist company. It may well be that we are in a transitional stage, where the fundamental nature of companies is about to change. Over the years I have had the opportunity to experiment with different forms of businesses, ones which did not own their own research or production, for example, or businesses which were purely production units, serving many different business masters. But nothing replaces the immediacy of the small, balanced team who are driving a business as fast as it can go in its own right. They may lack the ultimate in sophistication in the specialist functions, but they more than make up for this by being closer to the market, more responsive to the needs of their customers and quicker to adapt in every way. It is this pressure for speed of response and flexibility which is inexorably leading larger companies to try to break themselves down into different organisational forms. Practically every large company I know is seeking to emulate the advantages of small, compact businesses, whilst retaining the advantages of their own large size.

Unfortunately, whether we like it or not, there are many fields of business which can only be managed by large organisations. The sheer amount of resources that it is necessary to deploy in order to compete with the best in the world means that it is very difficult to be a world leading oil company if you are a small company. The inherent advantages which are available to very large organisations depend greatly upon extensive research and development skills. I have never believed that big is best, and for very many years I have believed, following Schumacher, that small is beautiful. The problem is that we need the advantages of size, together with the behavioural skills and adaptability that come with the small – which is an extremely difficult trick to turn. However, unless a large organisation is able to bring more to the party than the sum of its parts there is no justifiable business reason for being large. If a company is a heterogeneous collection of small, totally independent operations it is surely better that they are hived off to make their own way – the shareholders themselves may well be better off holding shares in fifty small companies than in one large one. Whatever a large company is able to bring to its individual parts there is one thing which it cannot bring and that is the exploitation of time. Large organisations, even if they manage to avoid the temptations of endless control systems, monolithic direction setting and continuous involvement in areas which are beyond their immediate realms of knowledge, are most unlikely to bring the attributes of speed and flexibility. It is a fact that the liner QEII cannot turn quickly, however it is also a fact that she has her own advantages, which smaller ships cannot match. Speed is only achieved by a continual feeling of urgency and a willingness to settle for something less than perfection in order to get on the road more quickly. I have been quoted as saying that I believe in speed rather than direction and, although one cannot follow that philosophy to its ultimate conclusion, the general thrust of the thought is right. Far too much time is spent in trying to ensure the absolute perfection of the decisions which organisations are going to take. In fact there is almost always a good degree of clarity and consensus about the general direction in which an organisation should be going. 'The best is the enemy of the good,' and those who seek to satisfy themselves that they have eliminated every risk and covered every possibility will usually be too late in the race.

Increasingly it seems that in the future we are all going to want more variety rather than less. Technically the cost of variety has been continuously reduced. Despite the pressures of international advertising and the ubiquity of media such as television, the people who constitute the world market are still, thank goodness, individuals rather than a homogeneous mass. When everybody has 'kept up with the Joneses', what do the Joneses do? People want different things and, even when they want the same sort of things, they want them presented or sold in different ways, or at least looking different. Elsewhere in this book I remarked that I do not believe that we are going to see very many 'Euro-products' because the history, cultural diversity, tastes, climatic conditions, methods of distribution and so on in each country are so different. Indeed I hope we do not see a continual trend towards sameness. The advances in large-scale production no longer necessitate producing everything the same. The days of Henry Ford, when you could have any colour you liked so long as it was black are long since gone and individuals wish to use their purchasing power to buy difference and express their individuality through variations of taste. Yet again the Japanese have shown the way. For many years now Nissan has been producing 'specials' in Japan. These have many more points of difference than the fancy paint trim and accessories which tend to mark the European special edition. They are deliberately limited in production numbers, in order to enhance their scarcity value, and are eagerly snapped up by the Japanese buyers. The fact that Toyota now make all their cars in Japan to order also means that it is possible to specify variations far outside the existing range of options which are the bread and butter of most car manufacturers. I believe this trend will increase as competitive advantage moves away from single large-scale production lines, and computer and other methods of control enable individual choice to find its way into the broader manufacturing market-place. These are the things which give the richness of choice which the developed world increasingly seeks.

For the businessman and manufacturer this means a continual search for the new and different, which comes on top of their age-old task of continuously trying to make more, of better, from less. I have been interested to observe the growth of the belief that the Japanese concept of 'Keizen', or continual improvement in every sphere of activity, is a new discovery. The job of the businessman has always been one of continuous and incremental improvement. The difference now is one of scale and speed. Whereas you used to be able to stay ahead by a modest but continual improvement in productivity there are now businesses, such as the semi-conductor business, where improvements in productivity of over ten per cent per annum are necessary just in order to survive. The common ground in all these approaches is the realisation that time and flexibility are sources of competitive advantage. But, like every facet of business, this realisation can only bear fruit in ways which ensure economic survival if the logic of the belief is followed inexorably through to its natural conclusion. We have to seek ways of getting there faster and, of course, we also have to be sure that we are heading in the right overall direction. Speed and flexibility are self-rewarding characteristics. Once we have a business organisation which is quickly adaptable, we can tack and veer faster than the competition in order to take advantage of opportunities that have turned up, or to correct errors of direction which we have made in our enthusiasm to get started down the line. I am aware that this philosophy appears to contradict my admiration of the way in which the Japanese think their way through things before actually starting into action but, provided that the same pressures for speed are applied to the thinking process as are applied to the action stages, I do not see a conflict. The reality is that the old adage 'more haste less speed' is still true. Sadly business people always feel happier when they are in action, rather than when they are sitting and planning what they are going to do, and how. However, the luxury of thinking about things and being sure that you have 'done your homework' before you actually press the button are not valid excuses for endless, unprofitable debate. Discussion and reiteration are necessary to gain commitment and clarity, but they need to be seen against a background of urgency and a sense of time. More often than not, the time spent in planning and gaining commitment to action is more than made up by the improved ability to work together and clarity of purpose when you actually set forth on your chosen path. But the essence of the whole thing has to be the feeling of urgency and the determination that it is in the speed and use of time that your company or business is going to seek its competitive advantage.

9 Where to Go in the Wild Wood

The earlier chapters of this book have outlined many of the changes that are happening now, and the pressures to which companies and businesses are reacting. I have written a great deal about ways of coping with external rates of change, and the characteristics which organisations will have to develop if they are to succeed. However, there is one inescapable responsibility of the top management of any business, and this is to decide the direction in which the business is going, and what I have called the vision. Plainly, as in all business matters, there is no single solution to this, and equally plainly this is the key decision on which your ultimate prosperity will depend. Even if you get the vision and direction right there are still an infinite number of things which can go wrong on the way, and I have pointed out some of them. Obviously the selection of the particular area which you are going to target is one of the most difficult ones. In selecting the forward focus of your business you need the greatest possible breadth of vision about the changes which are occurring around you. In any event, such is the rate and unpredictability of change that it is very difficult to forecast your direction absolutely correctly. However, it is readily apparent that if you get it absolutely wrong there may be disastrous consequences for everyone involved. There are a number of broad factors involved in charting your forward direction and selecting the nature of your business in the nineties which differ greatly from the eighties, and all these factors must be taken into consideration. Management is not about drifting and just reacting to external events – management and leadership are about doing one's best to envisage the probable trend of future pressures, and then charting a course which maximises the opportunities and minimises the risks. During the nineties it is almost inevitable that the risk profile of successful businesses will be heightened – if only because many of the forces which are at work will increase the chances of failure – which will be both swifter and more inexorable in the nineties than in the eighties.

In the eighties it was possible to survive (although perhaps not prosper) with a business which was run adequately well, but in the nineties this kind of performance will simply not be enough. It is rather like the whole question of quality. Adequate performance has now become the norm – just as quality is no longer a source of advantage. Companies that are to succeed will have to show wisdom, and their leadership will have to utilise the sort of helicopter vision to which I have referred so frequently. In order to achieve this it will be absolutely necessary for the top leadership of businesses to take a much broader perspective of the business trends and various external forces which are at work, since many of the assumed sources of economic advantage are no longer there. Sheer size is now no longer enough to render a company invulnerable, and neither is the possession of up-to-the-minute manufacturing or information technology. As a broad generalisation, the companies which survive are those which find ways of adding value – in all areas of their activities. This statement tends to induce a slightly panic-struck feeling of helplessness on the part of the traditional manufacturer. He has been struggling to improve his methods of production, his forms of organisation, the training and motivation of his staff and the financial management of his business, and a call to add further value seems like crying for the moon. The difficulty is that customers have such a large choice of suppliers that merely producing a consistently high quality product, at a broadly competitive price, is not going to sustain a business. The price will be under continual attack and your business has entered the sort of race which very rapidly becomes a zero-sum game. An example of this is the Double Two shirt company, which was the subject of a recent Troubleshooter programme. The company had continued to produce a high quality product at a competitive price – but it seemed to me that the product no longer had sufficient distinction to pick it out from the rest. In its early days the success of the company had been based on continual innovation and difference, and the fact that there was now so little apparently compelling need to buy a Double Two shirt was one of the factors which had led to its current state of problems.

The easiest way of adding value is to provide a service or solve problems. If you are manufacturing a product you are always working within a calculable cost of whatever it is you are making, so it is relatively easy to work out what the actual costs of any manufacturing process are. Once that is done buyers will continually press for erosion of the margin, until there is really nothing left in order to enable you to continue in business. However, it isn't only the buyers who will cause you headaches. Your competitors can also cost the product extremely accurately, by a process known as reverse value engineering, and can then set that as an example which they have to better if they are to overtake you on price. Any buyer or competitor can quite easily cost the item closely enough to destroy the profit margin, thereby causing you considerable headaches. However, when it comes to the solution of problems you are working in an altogether different field. The buyer will usually know what the problem is costing him, and the price which he is willing to pay is related to the savings to him, rather than the cost to you. A good example of this is the water treatment business. Every owner of a package boiler knows the enormous cost to him of having the boiler go off-line for one reason or another, and that cost will be uppermost in his mind. He will therefore be willing to pay for specialists continually to treat the water, in order to avoid at least one possible cause of problems. As a result continued cover is more likely to be maintained, which ensures that good prices can be obtained for the service he offers. Problems can often arise because of changes in competitive position, or come from unexpected areas. Most companies tend to keep a close watch on their immediate competitors, but it can be equally important to keep an eye on the strategies of people in totally disparate businesses, who may be viewing your own business as a source of future advantage. Canon was traditionally looked upon as a camera maker, rather than a supplier of office technology, Brother was looked upon as a sewing machine manufacturer – and so on. Competition in products can come from anywhere – and with a speed which any but the most flexibly organised company will find difficult to combat. Moreover, the newcomer in an area of manufacture almost always starts with advantages. He has brand-new technology and a brand-new production system, with newly trained people – unencumbered by the historical problems of the past. The world out there is an angry, unforgiving place. Often the danger comes from a newly emerging economic area or country. All too frequently those which are based in the Far East have the advantage of the highly focused governmental support which has been such a key factor in the growth of most of the East Asia dragons. Indeed it is this form of focused governmental support which has enabled East Asian countries to continue to compete, even when the advantages of cheap labour have long since vanished with time – as with Japan. Plainly it is an extraordinarily difficult thing to abandon the historical basis of one's business. After all, it is the area which you know – your people understand the market, you have your customer base and it is where you have served your apprenticeship. Diversification, in the sense of conglomerate companies, has a bad name and has gone greatly out of fashion in recent years. And yet diversification, in a step-out way from one's base, remains the key to longevity in companies.

In other books and other places I have written about the ephemeral nature of businesses as institutions. There are a surprisingly small number of companies which are a hundred years old or more. Although I know of one, which I believe to be the oldest company in the world, which is still in the printing business in which it started in the seventeenth century, the overwhelming majority of companies which survive are those that have continuously evolved and diversified away from their original core. This is the classic business situation – where you are damned if you do and you are equally damned if you don't. There are very few basic sources of business success which can be sustained indefinitely, and even then they can only be sustained by radical and far-reaching changes in technology and the ways in which the business works. But if diversification is to be successful it has to build on the strengths that the company already has. Senior managers easily deceive themselves about what the real strengths of the business are. All too often the real advantages that a company has are intangible ones, such as the skills of its people, but these skills can only be applied and utilised if they are focused into areas where they can show a particular advantage.

The key to future success lies in being a substantial player in whatever market you are in. The difficulty with this is that everybody then assumes that you have to be the world's largest and although this is highly desirable, it is still possible to be the world's largest business in an area in which the world-wide demand is relatively small. Large is a relative term, rather than an absolute one. For many years I have believed that large companies are very difficult to manage in a fast changing way. The future will increasingly lie with a company which finds its niche role in an area in which it can play world-wide, while still operating from a company base of a manageable size and utilising the full skills of all its people. There are companies – particularly in Germany – which have continued in the same line of business, in the same town, over many years and are still recognised as being the world leaders in their own field. It is noticeable for example that the world-leading Steiff soft toy business has remained in the town of its origin, and still specialises in making teddy bears or other toy animals. The key really is that you must be a power player in the niche which you choose. This niche does not necessarily have to be a world-wide one. There are a number of luxury products with very high mark-ups, which have established a cachet all of their own, where it is the possession of the branded item itself, be it a Rolex watch or a Louis Vuitton suitcase which is the unique selling proposition. Profitability in this sort of business is very high and the products do, indeed, sell throughout the whole world. Nevertheless there are surprisingly few products, except luxury ones, which sell in the same form throughout the entire world, and the niche is often of the sort of manageable size which even a small or medium sized company can hope to cope with.

Ideally companies should be looking at fields of endeavour which are of a manageable size and which are reasonably impervious to attack from other sources. The market for fresh fish, even with improvements in transport technology, is still a local market, but the market in fresh-cut flowers has become, in the most astonishing way, almost a global one. The flower grower is now competing with very high quality air-transported flowers from tropical and other countries, in a way which few professional flower growers had forecast or expected. It isn't enough merely to look at the market-place which exists today when one is trying to set one's company's course for the years ahead. It is necessary to use real creative imagination to visualise where the demand you are seeking to satisfy is likely to come from. It may be that other potential competitive sources have major advantages, such as the consistent climate in Australia or California, which has enabled them to mount an attack on the variable quality of wines which we are able to produce in Europe, with our more uncertain climate. Of course, taking such a broad-scale look at the world is not merely a matter of scanning the horizon for potential enemies. In essence what you are looking for are areas where you believe that your starting strengths give you a potential for expansion and growth on a broader world scene.

It is perfectly possible to sit down with a blank sheet of paper and devise an ideal business for yourself, in a brave new world, which you could seek to enter totally afresh – hiring new people and building up a business from scratch. By definition, however, this approach is extremely expensive, if only because of the time that will elapse before you have any positive cash flow and before you can establish any critical mass. It is probably safer to use your existing business as the base from which to evolve a further business, hopefully utilising the positive cash flow from your own business to set up the new. During the nineties it will be very difficult to develop any new businesses unless you have a ready source of cash to keep them supplied, since the current, and prospective, real costs of money are high. If it is to be able to service borrowed money and generate enough money to continue growing of its own accord, a business opportunity must be able to generate an extraordinarily high margin. Most current businesses can be turned into cash generators, if that is what is needed. In a field like publishing it is possible to turn a business into a cash generator by severely limiting the amount of new publications and relying upon the flow from the backlist, or alternatively entering a field such as educational publishing, where the backlist is all. Diversification as a step-out, based upon existing skills, market position, or service needs of your customers, is a relatively low-risk operation in the first place. If you start as a manufacturer you are trapped in a position where continuous improvement, and hence continuous investment in your manufacturing technology, will be necessary over the coming years. There are still plenty of manufacturing businesses which are cash generative but they still need to increase – or at least sustain and protect the margin, which can best be achieved by adding service to the products.

Some sources of service are, in themselves, less likely to be sources of sustainable competitive advantage, although they may well be sources of security of tenure. Despite the hazards and difficulties involved in it, the trend towards closer collaboration with customers and suppliers does mean that you are less likely to suddenly lose your primary position as an accredited supplier. It is absolutely essential to look at the chain of supply. However the idea that being able to supply consistent quality, on a 'just in time' schedule, is enough on its own to get, and hold, the business is, I believe, a fallacy. People now expect that element of service, just as they now expect consistently high quality. These things are almost a condition of business rather than sustainable sources of competitive advantage. Nevertheless there are still some services which the manufacturer can produce for his customer. The customer is as anxious to stay ahead in the race for novelty and cost saving as you are – being the most innovative supplier, with the best design standards, has real advantages in its own right. It can be helpful for your customer to feel that you are a team, so that he can be confident that it is as important to you as it is to him that he will not be taken by surprise by another competitor with a better form of packaging – or whatever it is that he buys from you. Being so close to your customer's business that you really understand what his problems are – and in some cases can seek to provide the solution before he is even aware that he has a problem – can be a real source of competitive advantage. Maintaining a successful business in the nineties will involve having these kinds of relationships with your suppliers as well as your customers. However, not all customers or suppliers are equal – and not all of them will survive this new, harsher environment. It is absolutely necessary to be as selective with your customers as you are with your suppliers. It is no use doing a large percentage of your business with an easygoing customer who is actually going to lose the competitive race; better by far to be in with the toughest, but fastest moving customer, whom you believe is likely to survive.

One of the snags about these links through the chain is that it is all too easy to come to believe that the chain is a single stage one at each level. Moreover, if you are a really good supplier your customer will be continuously pressing you for exclusivity, and placing demands on you which challenge your ability to supply. Even though a chain of totally exclusive suppliers and customers is more flexible than a wholly owned vertically integrated company, it is still likely to suffer the same forms of familiarity and decay. As a broad generalisation it is better to be a substantial player for each of your customers, rather than being the sole supplier – or only having a single outlet for your products. The companies which will succeed in the future are probably those which have two or three suppliers at each stage and which, in turn, supply two or three customers. This ensures that there will always be an element of competition, which is still the only way of keeping businesses sharp, fast moving and continuously alert for the necessity for change. A multiple, flexible chain of this sort does not betoken a lack of trust in its various links. Just as the wise businessman who finds himself in a monopoly situation will speedily try to introduce some competition into the market, so the wise operator in the nineties will avoid having all his eggs in one basket, as well as avoiding having too many baskets. A strategic approach of this sort places tremendous demands upon the conviction, fortitude and consistency of the leadership of the company. There is always the pressure to reinforce a good thing and to ensure, and apparently to optimise, the business at the expense of other competitors. Your chosen customers will be those who are recognised for their strength, price leadership, speed of reaction and their rate of introduction of new products and services. You in turn will try and bind yourself to them by finding more and more services to supply to them. You might be seeking to repair and service your equipment on the customer's own ground, for instance. I know of some excellent companies which have built their businesses entirely on the basis of 'managing' the total supply of a required service to another business, be it treated water, transport or distribution. The diversification of the British Oxygen Company into the chilled transport service, which carries out almost all the chilled transport for Marks & Spencer, is a good example of this sort of approach. The point is that the problem is taken away and the customers can sleep at nights, concentrating on their own basic business. These views about which are the key customers must be taken with long-term business cycles in mind.

Difficult though it is to believe at the time of writing this book, recessions do not go on for ever and even slumps are recovered from. The good customer is a customer who will succeed in living through the bad times and will enhance his position in the good times. It is too easy to follow the customer with whom the chemistry has been right from the word go – the 'chemistry' has to be made to be right with the customers who have the best future. However, it is very difficult indeed to sustain a long-term relationship with customers with whom you cannot communicate and in whom you do not have trust and confidence. You must seek a customer base whose business values and ideas are congruent with your own, always remembering that a supply chain is only as good as its weakest link. Although it is very comfortable to find people whose views are exactly the same as your own, what you actually need are people whose basic business values may be similar, but who surprise you by constant differences of viewpoint, approach and expectation. Good business is not comfortable business, good business is constantly striving to move faster and the optimum level of friction is not zero. People become easily concerned about differences of viewpoint and all too frequently allow emotion to take over. It is absolutely futile to think that customers can be bludgeoned into accepting your viewpoint. I have recently come across a surprising number of people who have believed that their customers can be forced to react in particular ways. Possibly an extreme example of this has been the banks, who have repeatedly carried out actions for their own administrative and commercial benefit, and expected that their customers would have to lump it. Even if it were possible to achieve this you could hardly have a worse basis for an ongoing business relationship. Resentment, and a feeling of antagonism, will inevitably grow and very soon the customer will be actively seeking to place his business elsewhere. Over-playing your hand through what you perceive as the uniqueness of your product or position has, in my experience, almost always been the road to future trouble. The objective throughout is to try to ensure that everyone who is involved prospers – because if they do there is something for you all to share. On occasions this will mean forgoing some of the perceived short-term profit or advantage in order to play for the long term. In tough, competitive times this is something which is extraordinarily difficult to do, and the people within your organisation may find it difficult to understand. There is a great urge in business to appear to be macho and tough and, far from being viewed as a good long-term businessman, the person who does not exploit his customers in the short term is often seen, within his own organisation, as being weak or having been in some way corrupted. Over the years the purchasing managers of super-markets have managed to establish an unenviable reputation for heedless bullying, irrespective of the effect on their suppliers. Indeed, there are many horror stories of rude and aggressive young buyers who do not care whether they run their suppliers out of business. There could barely be a greater contrast with long-term players like Marks & Spencer, who consider the loss of a supplier something to be deeply regretted. And yet the conditions of the nineties, with enhanced competition coming at you from every side, means that these relationships are of the greatest possible importance.

An added complication is that, increasingly, such relation-ships will be carried out across cultures and across countries. If you think you have problems relating to customers in your own country, try building up long-term relationships with business people from other environments, who start with totally different views, values, expectations and languages from your own. And yet the world is becoming a smaller place and the number of purely local markets, like that for fresh fish, is growing smaller all the time. If you are to become a significant player in your chosen field, it is almost inevitable that you will be operating in a wide range of countries, and in a wide range of languages. Here again absolute consistency and clarity as to the end objectives of your business are essential if you are to weather the inevitable problems of communication, misunderstanding, perception and so on. However the bright lining to the cloud is that each such problem that is overcome forms the basis for a better and more successful relationship for the future. Just as the cus-tomer whose complaint is dealt with effectively and sympa-thetically, surprisingly, often ends up being an extremely loyal customer, so difficulties overcome form a vital binding force for the future.

There is another trap in these flexible chains which must be looked for. It is highly probable that at some stage you and your people will be tempted to move forward and compete with your own customers. Perhaps there is dissatisfaction about your share of the cake, or a (very common) belief that the customer's world is cosier and more comfortable than your own, and it may well be. But you must be very aware of where you are heading. The path to verticalisation and inflexibility of operation is paved with the best possible short-term intentions, but the end point is still the same. Integrating forwards and taking out your customers, as well as being a hard battle, almost always gets the balance of the business wrongly focused and ultimately ends in tears. You really have enough to do making sure that your own business is developing fast enough. The point about these flexible chains is that no individual step in them must be regarded as immutable but, equally well, no individual link should be abandoned without careful, thoughtful testing – you must be absolutely clear about where you are going to be if you cut off.

These are additional reasons why clarity of thinking, consistency and commitment to the vision at every level of the organisation is a key to deciding the direction. During the nineties it is the companies which have a reasonably long-term consistency of vision about where they are going, coupled with tremendous tactical flexibility, and continuous experimentation at the fringes of their activities, which stand the best chance of surviving. Like everything else in business, this balance between concentration and tolerance of modest experimentation is an extraordinarily difficult one to manage. Nevertheless, it is very likely that many of the ways ahead will be found by people who are closest to the market-place, rather than the commander of the vessel, standing on the bridge scanning the world horizon. The commander should continuously encourage the 'lookouts' to peer around from their position of advantage, and he must be prepared to listen to them extremely carefully. You are looking for opportunities to spread out from the edges of your existing business, in order to reinforce those areas in which you are most successful. To do this it may be necessary to pull out of those areas which fail to fit in with the total picture, or stand the tests of competitive advantage. For every company that has won through by sticking obstinately to their conviction that their vision is right, one can point out many more examples of those who have gone down the pan through lack of willingness to change. These problems are always ones of balance. The combination of stickability and vision, together with enough flexibility to be willing to shift direction before disaster strikes, constitutes the real task of directional leadership. In making these decisions it is always necessary to look ahead, both at the most optimistic view of how things may evolve and the potential downside.

It is a source of constant surprise to me how many business people are prepared to stay with businesses which seem to me to have an unbalanced business profile. We all know the sort of business where, if everything goes right (and it seldom does), a modest return will ensue. The characteristics of such businesses are almost always that as soon as things begin to go wrong the business begins to incur horrific and continuing losses. When setting the direction for the future, it is important to have an understanding of this balance between potential risk and potential gain. It is not the slightest use having a splendid vision of the future if you cannot survive long enough to achieve it. Survival means having some 'steady little earners'. 'Steady little earners' are seldom particularly sexy, in a business sense, and indeed may not have the potential for future growth that is the aim of every business and investor. The investor is interested because he wants to see continuous capital growth, as well as the flow of dividends, while those involved in the business are interested in growth because with it come enhanced rewards and power – and that seductive feeling of success. The trick is to ensure that your business profile contains both types of business, and woe betide the company which goes solely for the seductive sounds of very high risk and very high potential reward. One of the major problems that affects the 'steady little earner' is that, all too often, those entrusted with the care and management of such desirable businesses became dissastified with their lot. It is not the world's most satisfying managerial task to run the company's cash cow, while others seem to throw the proceeds of one's cautious husbandry to the winds. And yet, time and again, you see the power that can be generated by a really good cash flow business. While arguments will continue for a great many years to come about the ethical aspects of the tobacco industry, the fact remains that tobacco companies are prodigious cash flow machines, which have made the growth of many attractive alternative growth areas possible. The 'steady little earners' are always likely to be in fields of business which have passed their growth phase, and where the weaker players have long since been gobbled up. It isn't always necessary to have an entirely separate field of business as a 'steady little earner'. Quite a number of companies have found themselves producing a range of products which meet the ongoing needs of consumers, and where a position of strength has been achieved over a number of years. The publishing of school textbooks has long been seen as a steady source of revenue which can enable publishers to take a 'flier' on other, riskier, ventures.

Somewhere within every business that is to survive during the nineties, there needs to be a basic source of relatively recession-proof cash flow earnings if the company's inevitable ambitions to be a winner in the nineties are to be achieved. A myriad of technology consultants and academic institutions have studied the problems of setting strategies, and they have produced a number of helpful ways of looking at business opportunities in order to enable the strategic decisions to be taken. None of them, however, can actually do the job for you. The leader of any business, be he a private owner, chief executive, or chairman of a large multinational company, has the twin responsibilities of setting the values for the business, and its direction and aspirations. All too often small businesses tend to set their sights at levels of achievement far beneath what they are really capable of. This may apply particularly to family businesses, which reach a 'comfort level' where the aspirations of the family are being met but where, in fact, there is still considerable potential in the business if it is to survive through further generations. A good example of this sort of approach is shown by the Morgan Car Company who, despite asking for assistance, really seemed content to leave things as they were, despite the very substantial unrealised potential for growing the business that still existed. This problem of aspiration applies just as much to the 'steady little earner' as it does to the more exciting growth aspect of one's business portfolio. Indeed, 'steady little earners' only remain 'steady', or indeed 'earners', if they themselves are subject to inexorable pressure continuously to improve the product, the quality, the margin and the service. One of the problems of business leadership in this directional sense is that it is all too easy to take one's eye off the basis of one's prosperity, in order to seek new and apparently more attractive and rewarding fields. This tendency is exacerbated by the wish of your brightest and best managers to work in areas of potential growth, rather than the more boring engine room of continued prosperity. This problem requires careful selection and placing of individuals within your company, so that you find those who are admirably suited to the engine room work, and others who are excellent at exploiting the opportunities of a new and growing business. It is seldom that managers are good at both of these fields simultaneously, but the board of the enterprise must be careful to nurture values which will support both types of activity. If the business is to survive and grow it is important to keep an eye on the allocation of resources between both types of activity and to watch the balance between the new and the old.

Of course, this is one of the reasons why organisations need the collective wisdom of a board and are, in turn, helped by the difference of perspective and viewpoint that non-executive board members can bring. Although the setting of direction involves every layer of the company, because it must be built upon the capabilities of the company and the art of the possible, the task of direction setting is uniquely the job of the board as a whole. Although this seems self-evident, it is surprising how cavalierly many boards take this responsibility. Fortunately more and more boards are prepared to spend the necessary time together to debate the strategy and continually to check and reassess it. These strategic discussions are, in my view, best held 'off site' and in more casual surroundings – where one can move away from the day-to-day din of the battle and try to step back and look at the business, the world horizons, the funding opportunities, the technological opportunities and so on in a more relaxed and open way. This process is almost a necessity of itself, because one has continuously to challenge and update one's own assumptions. Nothing is more difficult than reversing your own decisions, taken after a great deal of thought and consultation, and looking objectively at the strengths which one thought one had, which may not be standing up to the test of time. This is another area where external views both from the non-executive directors and, on occasions, consultants or specialists in the field which you are looking at, can be of real help. Almost by definition discussions about the future strategy and direction are painful ones, which involve a great deal of soul-searching and readiness to divorce self-sustaining internal myths from harsh reality. By definition strategies should not be changed too often. Even in today's tempestuous world one should be aiming at a forward strategy which will last five years or more. It is the tactics within the strategy which can vary continuously but, if the work on the strategy has been done correctly, you need reasonable consistency of purpose and objective in order to achieve the impact you are looking for. As I have pointed out elsewhere, even the best strategy will not succeed without the wholehearted commitment of all the people in the business to the strategic aim. The techniques for gaining this commitment are the ones which are outlined in Chapter Two. Having a clear strategic aim, a 'vision' of a better future, is an essential part of gaining the commitment to change. As I have pointed out, the major mechanism which will move people away from a reliance on the present is dissatisfaction with that present – together with a believable picture of a better world which they can aim at. That, after all, is what strategy is about. Lack of commitment to the strategy is as great a problem as having a totally wrong strategy. As in most things in business, perfection is not essential. A strategy which is eighty per cent right but which commands the support of your people is better than a strategy which, in purist terms, you may believe to be one hundred per cent correct, but which has the support of no one. The important thing, above everything, is to have a clear aiming point, which you can all accept as being a believable way ahead. No matter how great the commitment, it is almost impossible to win if the strategy is totally wrong. It is all too easy for boards to run companies aground but, just as there is seldom one perfect solution for anything, so there is seldom one perfect stratagem. The strategy has to be one which is broad enough to command the support and seize the hearts and minds of the people who will have to execute it; it has to be carefully balanced for risk; it has to be possible, but stretching; and it has to be based on realistically high aspirations. It has to take a view about the totally unpredictable changes that may occur during its life and about the likely developments of the competition – who will be having the very same sort of debate, about the very same sort of difficulties. Surely, when so much rides upon it, this should be seen as the top responsibility of the most experienced business people in the whole outfit.

10 The Order of Battle

By definition the nineties are going to show many further changes in our ideas about organisation of business and business structures. Organisation should always be a function of the task which you wish to achieve, and should change constantly. Plainly organisation has many different objectives – some companies require methods of control and the avoidance of mistakes, whilst others are looking for speed. Obviously these require totally different types of approach. The characteristics of business in the nineties are going to be so different from those of the eighties that it would be surprising if the same forms of organisation were appropriate. There are also other forces at work. There are major public and shareholder concerns about the control of companies, personified by Robert Maxwell's activities, which are leading to pressures, and in some cases legal changes, which can involve different models of organisation at the top. One of the perennial arguments in business has always been about organisational behaviour. Many profess to believe that organisation affects behaviour, whilst the behaviourists insist that behaviour will always triumph over even the worst organisation. There is an element of truth in both arguments, but I believe that businesses work best where the organisation and the behaviour are mutually self-reinforcing. After all, in practically every business one is trying to channel the latent energy of all one's employees in order to achieve the commercial aims. This is always difficult, even with total clarity of objectives and with a vision which can command hearts and minds. It is unfortunately true that there is little general confidence or trust in commercial organisations. People are continuously looking for actions or forms of behaviour which give the lie to the words with which the aims and objectives of companies have been set out. Any mismatch between the values that are espoused and the organisational set-up is seen as giving further weight to the argument which says 'they don't mean what they say'.

As I have pointed out several times in this book, the major feature of the nineties with which businesses are having to contend is a frightening and constantly accelerating rate of change. In turn this means that the organisational forms to be adopted must be flexible ones, which can adapt to external change. Almost every business has set itself the aim of trying to produce 'a learning organisation'. This is a sort of commercial 'philosopher's stone' which, to the best of my knowledge, nobody has yet achieved. One of the difficulties is that almost everyone inherently dislikes change and yearns for stability, confidence and predictability. There is, therefore, an in-built conservatism in companies, which makes even managed change difficult to achieve. A learning company would be one in which the process of change continued as a self-driven fact, and the lessons of crude experience were continuously digested, analysed, recycled and turned into different patterns of behaviour – without enforcement from the top management. Just as all too few of us have the self-discipline continuously to learn and adapt in our private lives, so companies find this even more difficult. Even the process of analysis of achievement and mistakes is difficult, for companies tend to be quick to punish errors, and therefore few people are keen to wash their dirty linen in public – even if they have the intellectual honesty to confess to the blunders they have made. The mere mention of the word 'mistake' is enough to produce bristles of indignation and a violently defensive reaction from most people. Small wonder, therefore, that the learning organisation remains a dream rather than a practical reality.

In this chapter I have not sought to prescribe an ideal form of organisation for the nineties, but rather to list the trends in organisational thinking, behaviour and practice which need to be taken into account when setting up one's order of battle for the future. Sadly, there is all too little experimentation in organisation within businesses. In most businesses there is a remarkable degree of intolerance of organisational difference – despite the fact that it is self-evident that the type of organisation which is necessary in order to run a cash generating business should, by definition, be quite different from the type of organisation which is required for a business which is restlessly seeking out niche opportunities in the markets of the world. People still seem to feel that every company should have a subsidiary board or something similar – even though it is self-evident that a 'cash cow' business should have the lowest possible overheads, fewest possible chiefs, and minimum number of diversions from its ruthless pursuit of increased operational efficiency and reduction of costs. Moreover, organisations tend to evolve from a combination of the way in which things have always been done, the people who are available and their individual limitations or strengths. Although much time is spent debating organisational forms, it is often the area where there is the least lateral thinking. Indeed, as a broad generalisation, many of the concepts of industrial organisation still stem from old military forms of command – which could hardly be more inappropriate to business success. Even Alfred Sloane's concepts of staff and line had their origins in military organisation. However, military organisation is a relatively simple problem, the enemy is clear – as is the vision. The presence of the enemy is a powerful reinforcer to the discipline of one's own people, and there is not too much difficulty in diverting the attention from internal squabbling to fighting for one's life. In business the enemy is never clear – indeed tomorrow's competition or threats are all too likely to come from totally unexpected areas. The vision is seldom clear and, even when it is, is not always compelling enough to command hearts and minds. To my mind the differences between business and military thinking are so wide that I find it amazing that so much of military thinking has been adapted to business uses. The organisation of a business remains the prime responsibility of the board, and it is the task of the chairman or chief executive to ensure that enough time is spent discussing whether the organisation, and its constituent sub-organisation, is appropriate to perform the tasks which the board is setting. Such discussions are best held in an informal setting, and they should free themselves from the tyranny of the organisational chart. This kind of chart does have a real role in demonstrating the clarity of what has been set out in a pictorial sense. However, the systems which are most appropriate to cope with the complexities with which most businesses are struggling seldom lend themselves to such total clarity. A certain amount of 'fuzz' is almost inevitable if sufficient flexibility is to be built into the system to enable continual adaptation to occur. All this has similarities with the problems of optimisation to which I referred in an earlier chapter. Total organisational clarity and lack of ambiguity anywhere rapidly become a straitjacket, which acts as a brake, induces continual internal stress and, by its very rigidity, tends to punish experimentation, risk taking and speed. The fact that many managers dislike organisational difference is, in many cases, related to a lack of confidence that their people will do the 'right thing'. I have always found this very curious, since anyone who has worked in business of any sort knows that, in addition to the formal organisation, which presumably somebody somewhere fondly believes actually exists, the realities of day-to-day living are controlled by an informal organisation which is the product of experience and the determination of the company's employees to overcome the organisational controls and rigidities in order to be able to do their job. The truth is that nobody wants to work for an under-performing company – and if companies insist on people doing stupid or unnecessary things they will continually find ways round them. Nowhere was this demonstrated to me more clearly than in the field of work study, when I first joined industry in the 1950s. No matter how perfectly the work-study practitioner recorded the best current practice and, with the aid of method study and a host of other analytical tools, analysed the perfect way to do something, human ingenuity found ways to change and improve it. All of us accept the necessity for continuous improvement in the ways in which business is conducted, and we all know that nothing has ever been created which cannot be improved, and yet we seek to constrain these highly desirable aims by imposing endless systems. We seek to define jobs by job descriptions and responsibilities in the most detailed possible way, while at the same time continuously pressing for change and improvement. We need to apply the same yearning for productivity that we apply to production systems to the human systems which we set up. I therefore suggest that the organisation and the behavioural concepts which under-pin your business require regular review, in order to ensure that they are not becoming totally set in concrete.

Continuous organisational change is all too frequently described as chaos – and certainly it can be pretty untidy. Nevertheless a certain amount of 'chaos' or, as I prefer to describe it, 'organisational space', is required in any business if there is to be room for individuals within the business to grow and find other ways of achieving the required objectives. Instead of 'job description' I have always preferred the concept of 'aim' or 'objective' descriptions. It seems to me that the businesses which will prosper will have absolute clarity of long term vision and aim, and maximum flexibility in tactics, and it should be the same with organisations. Organisations should be living things – rather like the human body, where cells are continuously dying and being replaced by others. These replacements will be subtly different, or will relate to one another in different ways, for organisational forms have to evolve if they are to be relevant and appropriate to constantly changing business objectives. The prizes in the nineties will go to the companies which can change fastest, organise themselves flexibly, and yet retain the essential clarities that are needed to focus effort.

Personally I am not a great believer in organisational rules, by which I mean concepts such as 'span of control' etc. The fact is that each of us has seen examples of someone who can adequately control, with an appropriately light touch, as many as fifty people – and other individuals who have difficulty managing five. Organisation charts which have total symmetry, so that nobody has more than five direct reports, strike me as being further invitations to rigidity – rather than adaptability. Despite this, there are some things which are absolutely necessary within any organisational concept. Perhaps the most important of all is that every individual in a business should have one person who is responsible for advising, coaching, rewarding and developing them. Indeed, the biggest change in organisational thinking is the welcome concept that the boss is no longer the supervisor responsible for overseeing the detail of your work, but is the coach, back-up, mentor and friend. Most of us have recognised over many years that our best bosses were almost always those who never appeared to 'interfere' but were always there, in some miraculous way, just as we were becoming totally confused and lost. They always seemed to be one jump ahead and we tended to attribute this to their superior experience, rather than attributing it to their leadership skills.

Few organisations in the nineties are going to be able to

afford to have layers of supervision or wasteful regiments of co-ordinators. The pressure on costs alone makes these luxuries which are far too expensive to be tolerated in the future. There are other reasons for the extinction of these hangovers from the past. Since one of the prime needs for the nineties is speed, an organisation which has too many layers and too many people starts the race with horrendous handicaps which will be extremely difficult to overcome. The reasons for pressing for organisational change are as much to do with speed as they are with expense. We are all familiar with the current trend towards non-hierarchical organisation and indeed the words have become almost a religion in their own right. However one man's non-hierarchical organisation is another man's long, involved and rigid hierarchical set-up. If you start with fifteen layers between the shop floor and the man at the top, a reduction to nine seems like an unbelievably flat set-up. Equally these are things about which it is possible to kid yourself. A well-known international company set up a concept of 'three by three', so that each individual had responsibilities which were monitored from three organisational directions – geography, market and technology – and in turn each of these had no more than three layers. However you looked at it any individual at the bottom of that lot was still responding to nine people – it was merely the way they had been laid out which apparently reduced the numbers of those who were bearing down upon him. As in everything else in business, there is no unique and single solution which can be applied uniformly to every company.

However, there are some principles which can be applied in drawing up organisations, and some concepts which may be of help. I feel quite strongly about one principle, which is that there should never be an organisational layer unless it is achieving some identifiable added value. This is best approached from the top down, rather than the bottom up. If you start by asking yourself what the role of the chairman is and what only he can do, and then relentlessly push everything down – following that by what only the board can do, restricting board members to the unique job that only the board itself can do, and resolutely refusing to allow them the luxury of interfering and intervening in jobs which can be done below that level – you will speedily find that you are reducing the number of layers and, equally importantly, reducing the lateral numbers of people involved in each layer. There will always be a job for the man at the top, but there can be vast differences between what the job involves when running an enormous international company like ICI – which has a multiplicity of people and products and operates in practically all the countries of the world – and the operation of a company running a steam laundry in a small provincial town. Nevertheless, there are common factors in any size of organisation, and these represent the minimum, so to speak, that the chairman has to do. Any chairman of any board anywhere has the prime responsibility for the management, selection, training and development of the members of the board, and the organisation of the work of the board so that it is attuned to the achievement of clear objectives. The responsibility of the board is much more than merely to monitor and supervise the activities of those beneath it. Though monitoring and supervision are satisfying, relatively simple, undemanding and risk-free tasks, they tend to be elevated to the prime concern of those at the top of the company. Even if that were appropriate in some bygone age it is certainly not appropriate for the days ahead. The unique task of the chairman and the board is firstly to ensure, if the company is a large and disparate one, that it adds up to more than the sum of its parts; secondly to set the long-term vision and aspiration for the business; and thirdly to set the organisation, values and tempo of the business. In addition, the chairman or chief executive has the inescapable responsibility of representing the company's public face, both externally and internally. In doing this they must exemplify the values which the company claims to embrace. It is totally impossible to tell people that part of the values of the company is that it should be open and risk taking if the chairman himself is as closed as a clam – and cautious to boot. If the chairman really does represent that unfortunate combination, and the board truly believes that openness and risk taking are the key to competitive success, then they need to replace him.

In a business sense the primary goal for the nineties has to be to make an organisation more than the sum of its individual parts. In itself, organisational design has to add value to the unco-ordinated efforts of the mass of individuals who comprise a business. All too often organisational structures actually detract from the commitment and energy of the whole. Almost every business which carries out this 'value added' approach will end up with a satisfyingly small number of levels, and a manageable number of people at the top. It is of the greatest possible importance that the 'value added' exercise be done from the top down, rather than the bottom up. If you approach the exercise from the bottom up it is all too easy to persuade yourself that the person at the bottom cannot possibly take on all the responsibilities that could rightfully be theirs, and this is really a recipe for adding layers, rather than reducing them. However, even when you have got the number of layers right and have begun to approach the problem of the number of people, you still have the difficulty of how to enable them to relate to each other and how to form the ubiquitous organisational chart which you fondly believe will be the map of your enterprise. Here there are a host of experiments and ideas being carried out in various parts of the world, and a feature of all of them is to try to give space. They range from concepts such as concentric organisation, outlined by Professor Shoshana Zuboff, right the way through to organising for chaos, as exemplified by Tom Peters on the same subject. At the heart of the concentric organisation lies the belief that information technology has changed the way in which companies work. The major actions are taken by what are described as the 'knowledge workers', who we would recognise as being the shop-floor workers. These are the people who form the outer circle of the organisation. They actually carry out most of the operations for the business, more or less without supervision, co-ordinating their efforts by means of a fully open network of information technology. The intermediate ring of the concentric organisation is what we would describe as middle management. Their job is primarily to act as coaches and reinforcers of the knowledge workers at the rim. At the centre is a tiny core of people who are concerned with the strategic direction of the whole organisation. It is almost impossible to draw a concentric organisation in conventional organisational chart form. Organising for chaos takes the view that there should be almost no fixed organisation at all, and that practically everything in a business is accomplished by continuously shifting variable task forces who assemble to do a job, and then reassemble in a different way. These are extremes – but we are going to see much more experimentation and variability in the way that such organisations are set up.

When drawing up future organisational frameworks it is essential to bear in mind the strategic aims which you are trying to achieve, together with the external environment in which the organisation will be operating. Obviously it takes some time to get the organisation in place and operating. Everybody who has worked in any company knows that the way things work in practice and the organisational chart are seldom the same thing. A sort of unofficial organisation has almost always been developed over time, which finds the short cuts and tests the balance of power, and this will be constantly changed by the people who actually have to get the work done. The wise board will constantly look for the unofficial organisation and for those people who feature largely in it. It is on these movers and shakers that the company's future competitiveness will depend. One of the aims of organisational change is to remove the impediments which the unofficial organisation has sought to get around. This should release energy within the company to deal with the real problems outside – rather than trying to overcome the self-imposed constraints and limitations which the company has developed within itself. It has been said that good people can operate within almost any type of organisation. More depends upon the quality and motivation of the people than on the organisational form. Nevertheless, there is a big difference between a system of organisation merely being something within which one operates, and its actually being helpful, supportive and encouraging, therefore enabling energy and time to be focused on the main problem.

The competitive environment in the nineties will punish rigidity and slowness in organisation more harshly than in the past. Unless you are able to concentrate all the individual efforts and abilities of your employees in order continuously to improve all parts of your business, it will simply not survive. As I have tried to point out elsewhere, there are remarkably few areas of sustainable competitive advantage which will enable a business to overcome lack of focus in this way. Even the possession of an inviolable patent will no longer have quite the same competitive strength. Obviously anything unique which is protected by patent will still be a formidable competitive advantage, but companies which are lucky enough to possess such advantages will still have to work hard to organise and motivate their people, however, if they are to survive once the patent itself runs out. Moreover, technology is moving so fast that other ways will very frequently be found of achieving the same results, perhaps through an entirely different technological route – so the patent holder can seldom afford to rest on his laurels. It is my belief that organisational structures need to be flat, non-hierarchical, easily adjustable and designed to reinforce and assist both the achievement of the strategic aims and the motivation of your people. Although practically everybody at the bottom of a hierarchy would agree with me, it is surprising how tenaciously those at the top or middle of an organisation like to hang on to the status quo. It gives an enviable sense of belonging and certainty about where you are and what your validity in a company is, but it proliferates work and loses time. Hierarchical achievement has often been used as the substitute for reward – particularly in Britain. Perhaps this has something to do with the absence, until recently, of very large material rewards. One has only to look at the way in which public service motivates people by moving them up an ever stretching hierarchy of jobs, to see that it has been considered to be cheaper to produce new job titles than to differentiate performance by individual rewards. The difficulties with hierarchies are, of course, that they increase the number of people who can say no and decrease the number of people who can say yes. They remove more and more individual responsibility from the people who are actually doing the job, and enable the game of passing the parcel up the line to be played endlessly within an organisation. All of this removes your people from the immediacy of the battle, and from the feeling of deep personal involvement and commitment. Ultimately, competition in the nineties depends more and more upon the battle between the equality, brainpower, imagination and focus of your team, and the competition's team. In the past business success has depended very largely upon the quality of the people that you can engage and motivate, and this will be even more the case in the future.

In the nineties the big difference is that very few businesses will use people as replacements for machines. If the only way of doing the job is by hand, inevitably the business will either migrate to the lowest cost area or, alternatively, to the highest skill area. Practically all the competition will be between the intelligence of everyone in your business, pitted against the skill, intelligence and commitment of your competitors. Ultimately the only source of sustainable competitive advantage is your people and the values and motivation systems of your business. We all know that, just as in every other facet of life, the best attracts the best – and that any business is either spiralling upwards or spiralling down. Not only must any business set its sights on selecting the very best, but once having selected them it must also concentrate on the problems of developing their skills and abilities, heightening their aspirations, and continuously motivating them to do better. People actually enjoy being stretched and gain confidence from the experience of continuous growth. Moreover, a good track record in employing and motivating the very best is an enormous source of attraction to good quality people, and so the virtuous circle reinforces itself.

Similarly if you have the organisational and motivational set-up wrong – so that people are disenchanted and spend much of their time complaining about the organisation itself – you will find that it is the very best of your people who will be first to leave. By definition they are the ones who will find it easiest to obtain attractive employment elsewhere, and so the spiral of decline reinforces itself, with disastrous effects for the future. I have never believed in substantial differences in the abilities which people are born with. The majority of differences occur because people develop and are educated at different rates and therefore we see them at different stages of their growth to their ultimate potential. However, it is important that everyone is encouraged to make continuous efforts at growth and self-improvement. These habits are not in-born – rather they are responses to expectations laid upon us through our education and by our bosses and mentors on our journey through life. It is no accident that certain companies have a reputation for producing a disproportionate number of the outstanding managers of their day. Ford's system of training its financial people has offered prodigious numbers of managers the essential grounding which has enabled them to succeed in totally different fields of activity. Similarly, Shell, ICI and Marks & Spencer have long been recognised as excellent business schools in their own right. Such a reputation is of immense help in recruiting new employees. Even when, as appears to be the case in the early part of the nineties, there are more able people looking for positions than there are available positions, a well-deserved reputation for hiring and growing the best can only be of assistance to a company. All too often businesses forget that selection is a two-way process. Not only is the company choosing its future manager, but the employee is choosing his future career, as well as the place where he hopes to learn to apply and develop his skills.

Organisational systems can all too easily restrain the imagination and capability of the people who work in the company. For many years I have believed that most organisation and control systems are upside down, and I am now totally convinced that most of them are inappropriate for the conditions of the nineties. Organisational systems have habitually been about control and stopping people doing things. They have been about lack of trust, perceived minimisation of risk, endless supervision and grudging delegation of authority. The conditions of the nineties demand exactly the reverse. They demand risk taking, within a framework which will stop the inadvertent 'bet the company' type of risk. Contrary to popular belief, risk taking is not a natural, in-born quality. Some people find taking a risk easier than others, but almost no one naturally takes risks the whole time. Risk taking needs to be carefully considered, and balanced between the perceived opportunity and the consequences of failure, but it can only take place within an organisational framework which not only enables risks to be taken but actually encourages them. It is interesting that we so often choose to define risks as a responsibility, and the intermix of the two words gives an almost inevitable feeling that risk should be avoided. Our reward systems, our behaviour and our organisational structures all tend to discourage people from stretching themselves and taking risks. Yet, unless we are continuously pushing ourselves so that we are a little bit frightened, how are we ever going to extend our capabilities? Muscles only strengthen by being continuously pushed to their limits, and it is the same with people. People must be encouraged to go to the limits of their own self-belief, and only by so doing can they embark upon the moving staircase of continual improvement.

Organisations and leadership have to provide this 'crawling peg' of expectations, but such a 'crawling peg' depends upon praise and recognition of achievement, whilst at the same time asking for that extra effort for the next lap. I have operated within organisations which are very slow to praise, but very quick to demand an extra effort. I believe that people give of their best when they receive plenty of recognition for the effort they have made, whilst being encouraged to use their achievements as the basis for a renewed step-out towards a more distant goal. Training managers is exactly like training sportsmen. They need constant praise, but must never be allowed to feel that they have 'got there' – there is always another hill to climb, and in the nineties the hills will become higher and tougher at a terrifying rate.

In these chapters I have tried to set out some of the factors which make the present decade so very different from previous decades of my business experience. They are even more demanding, more competitive, and quicker in every way than the past decades. The rewards for success are there, just as they were in the past, but as the race gets faster there is less and less room for anything but top quality contestants. The vital importance of business success for all of society means to say that, increasingly, it will be businessmen and women who will be the chosen champions of their countries. On their success or failure will depend the well-being of all of us. Business life is becoming frighteningly more complex, and placing greater and greater demands, not just upon those fortunate enough to be business leaders but upon men and women at every level in an organisation. We should consider ourselves well served that there are so many people in the UK who have the ability to be top-flight managers and business leaders. However, no one can become a world champion without continuous study, effort, training and commitment. There is nothing God given which makes any particular country have a definitive or leading position in the race for business leadership. Let us never forget that in many ways we founded the industrial age. It is important that we re-create the same positions in world leadership that, as a nation, we enjoyed then. I am positive that we can do it again today, in many areas of our activities.

I hope very much that this highly personal perspective on why things are going to be so different will be of some help and assistance to the businessmen and women of the generations which will have to carry the banner for the next decades. Over the past years I have seen a surprising number of them, and those that I have met give me every confidence and belief that they can rise to the challenge – daunting though it may be. They deserve the support and admiration of us all – for it is on their abilities that all our futures depend.

*Also by John Harvey-Jones
and available from Mandarin*

GETTING IT TOGETHER
Memoirs of a
Troubleshooter

'*Sir John is that rare animal, a businessman who makes
business exciting . . . No businessman has ever written a
memoir like it.*'
SUNDAY TIMES

Sir John Harvey-Jones is one of Britain's most
admired businessmen. His television series,
Troubleshooter, with its clear-sighted look at ailing
British companies, became a national talking point,
and as chairman of ICI he topped the *Sunday Times*
poll of captains of industry five years running.

Getting it together is the memoir of a remarkable man
– and a fascinating account of the experiences that
made him a hugely successful manager.

Rich in illuminating anecdotes, this is a memoir
everyone working in an organisation should read.
Frank, beguiling and full of the wisdom about people
and business that has informed his working life, this
is the autobiography of the year.

A Selected List of Business Titles

While every effort is made to keep prices low, it is sometimes necessary to increase prices at short notice. Mandarin Paperbacks reserves the right to show new retail prices on covers which may differ from those previously advertised in the text or elsewhere.

The prices shown below were correct at the time of going to press.

☐	7493 0641 6	**Getting It Together**	John Harvey Jones	£5.99
☐	7493 1404 4	**Under the Hammer**	Andrew Davidson	£5.99
☐	7493 1487 7	**For Whom the Bell Tolls**	Jonathan Mantle	£5.99
☐	7493 1026 X	**Billion-Dollar Battle**	Matthew Lynn	£5.99
☐	7493 1138 X	**The Bundesbank**	David Marsh	£6.99
☐	7493 1362 5	**Junk Bond Revolution**	Fenton Bailey	£6.99
☐	7493 1024 3	**How to Succeed in Selling**	Alfred Tack	£4.99
☐	7493 0355 7	**New Realities**	Peter Drucker	£4.99
☐	7493 1342 0	**Measure Up!**	Dominic Hobson	£5.99
☐	7493 0840 0	**The Inner Game of Selling Yourself**	James Borg	£5.99
☐	7493 0859 1	**How I Multiplied my Income and Happiness in Selling**	Frank Bettger	£5.99
☐	7493 0578 9	**How I Raised Myself from Failure to Success in Selling**	Frank Bettger	£5.99
☐	7493 0459 6	**101 Ways to Boost Your Business Performance**	John Fenton	£4.99
☐	7493 1042 1	**So You Think You Can Manage?**	Video Arts	£5.99

All these books are available at your bookshop or newsagent, or can be ordered direct from the publisher. Just tick the titles you want and fill in the form below.

Mandarin Paperbacks, Cash Sales Department, PO Box 11, Falmouth, Cornwall TR10 9EN.

Please send cheque or postal order, no currency, for purchase price quoted and allow the following for postage and packing:

UK including BFPO — £1.00 for the first book, 50p for the second and 30p for each additional book ordered to a maximum charge of £3.00.

Overseas including Eire — £2 for the first book, £1.00 for the second and 50p for each additional book thereafter.

NAME (Block letters) ....

ADDRESS ....

....

☐ I enclose my remittance for ....

☐ I wish to pay by Access/Visa Card Number ☐☐☐☐☐☐☐☐☐☐☐☐☐☐☐☐

Expiry Date ☐☐☐☐